MW01283131

GOD IS NOT DONE WITH YOU YET!

STORIES OF GOD'S

DELIVERANCE AND

RESTORATION

AROUND THE WORLD

Pastor! God bless you.
There is no loss in serving God.
Joshua 1:8

PASTOR JOSEPHINE MUKAMAZIMPAKA

Dedication

I dedicate this book to those who have significantly impacted my life and helped shape me into the woman of God that I am today:

To my father and best friend, Bugingo Clever.

To my spiritual father and mother, Dr. Joseph and Freeda Serwadda—thank you for your obedience to the call of God upon your lives.

To my sweetest husband, Fred—thank you for being my covering. I am so grateful that God chose you to be my husband.

To my sweet girl, Josie—I love you so much. I know the hand of God is upon your life, and I can't wait to see the woman God has created you to be.

To Pastor Sharon Daugherty—thank you for all you did for me while I was under your leadership. You made my dreams come true! You are in my heart always.

To my dearest friend, Nadia.

To my spiritual daughter, Yana Ogor—you are my family.

To my favorite podcast hostess, Sarah Nardella—I cherish our friendship.

To my covenant brother, Christian Hedegaard, and his beautiful wife, Karen—it has been an honor and a privilege to serve alongside you for the past 28 years in ministry. You are my family. I love you.

Table of Contents

Continued on the next page

Introduction

People seem to give up on God very easily because they get offended, they have been abused, or they do not believe God is near them. How do you help people who have been betrayed? How do you help those who have been knocked down to rise again? I've seen many who were brokenhearted asking where God was during the tragedy.

My country, Rwanda, went through a genocide. After the genocide, many lost their families. The people they loved or who loved them were gone, and they seem to give up on God very easily because they get offended, they have been abused, or they do not believe God is near them. How do you help people who have been betrayed? How do you help those who have been knocked down to rise again?

When you try to tell them about God, no one wants to believe it. I heard people say over and over, if God is real, where was he during the genocide? Why didn't he save us from trouble? How could God let this happen to me? What have I done to deserve this? Every time I hear a question like this, it pierces my heart because I understand that pain. Twenty of my family members were buried alive. I had to dig up their bodies in the dark of night to give them a proper grave. So when I hear those questions, I have to take a moment to find my strength. Then, I start by saying what I know to be true. There is one way to come out of this. It is to forgive one another and believe Jesus as the Savior.

People often say I cannot forgive; I cannot let go. But if you don't, you will kill yourself in other ways. You will cause yourself to suffer for the rest of your life. You'll die from missing your family and from the anger. Anger blinds you. You'll stop being able to see good things; soon, the only thing your anger will let you see is revenge. You'll crave revenge, but oftentimes, you'll have no power to do it. The third way you'll die is from fear. As you see others suffering, you start to believe that you're not special. If you're not more special than your family, your friends, or your neighbors who were killed, then you believe whatever took them could take you as well. That's when you lose your confidence.

Have you experienced those feelings of unforgiveness, anger, or fear? Have you lost your faith in God? Let me encourage you. Do not fight with God about the things that happen. It is the world that betrays you. And after you are betrayed by everyone and everything, the only person left in the world who cares for you is God.

When Moses died, all of Israel thought their lives ended with Moses. He was their leader. The one who heard from God on their behalf. They didn't know where to go or what to do without his instruction. God looked down on them and saw how frustrated the people had become, so he called Joshua to be their new leader. In Joshua 1:5-6, God gives Joshua a message of encouragement and victory. He says,

> *No man shall be able to stand before you all of the days of your life. Just as I was with Moses, so I will be with you. I will not leave you or forsake you. Be strong and courageous, for you shall cause these people to inherit the land that I swore to their fathers to give them.*

God reminds the people in this verse that Moses' death was not the end for them.

As you read through the stories in this book, I hope it becomes apparent to you that the love of Jesus can conquer the despair and anger that causes you to be frustrated and depressed. Jesus can create in you a pure and clean heart filled with love and joy. In Galatians 5, it talks about the fruit of the Spirit being love and joy. When you're filled with love and joy, where will the anger live? No matter what happens, you'll live with a smile and be a blessing to others as well.

Chapter 1

My Childhood

My parents were Rwandan refugees. During the first genocide of 1959, they fled to Uganda. My father was a fashion designer, and my mother stayed at home to take care of the family. When I was conceived, I had six older sisters and two older brothers. My father did not want another girl. He wanted a boy. The day I was born was the day their marriage fell apart. My mother left our home and took me with her to her parent's house. She cared for me until I was nine months old. Then her parents insisted I be taken back to be raised with the rest of my siblings.

Peter and Cecelia Bugingo, my father and mother.

I was raised by my stepmother and grandmother. My grandmother died when I was seven years old. She was my best friend. She treated me like a princess. My grandmother gave me all the love and attention that anyone could ever desire. When she passed away, I began to miss my mother. I realized that there was a void in my life.

Suicidal Thoughts

Soon after my grandmother's death, thoughts of suicide began to consume my mind. I had been abandoned by my mother and rejected by my father. The last person whom I felt I could rely upon, my grandmother was gone as well. I felt alone. I lost the person whom I loved most. I lost my best friend.

When I Almost Lost My Life

Oftentimes, Satan knows the calling God has placed on our lives before we are aware of it ourselves. When I was nine years old, the devil made an attempt to completely destroy my life because he wanted to stop the call of God on my life. 1 Peter 5:8 says,

Be sober-minded; be watchful. Your adversary, the devil, prowls around like a roaring lion, seeking someone to devour.

One quiet morning, around 6 am, I went outside as usual to milk the cows. As typically done when milking a cow, I tied a rope around its legs to keep it from kicking me. While I was milking, one of the other cows turned around and bumped the cow I was milking, and it lost its balance. It fell on top of me! I passed out. When I woke up, I did not know where I was except that I was surrounded by people who were happy to see I was alive. It was difficult to breathe and stand. The pain was excruciating. My family tried to treat my injuries, but it didn't work.

From that day on, I lived in terrible pain. I couldn't lift anything heavy. Holding a cup to drink was terrible. One of my ribs was broken and had pierced my organs internally. Every time I was hungry, it felt like it was scratching my organs. I'd spend the whole day using one hand to hold my broken rib while I was talking to people. It was so tough that if I wanted to put something on the stove, I couldn't carry it alone. I'd have to wait for someone to come and carry it for me. The pain was in my head and all over my body, and I couldn't do anything about it. It felt like I was constantly being scratched on the inside. It caused a terrible constant headache. I tried to commit suicide because I was so tired of living my life in pain. I decided that I would end my pain once and for all.

One evening, while I was home alone, I located a bottle of poison, which was typically used as an insect repellent. I had no intention of repelling away any creepy critters; rather, I had every intention of taking my own life. As I lifted the bottle to take a sip, the bottle flew from my fingertips and shattered all over the bedroom floor. It felt as though someone had physically knocked it out of my hand. No one else appeared to be present, but something or someone prevented me from achieving my desired fate. The fumes from the bottle began filling the house quickly. Startled, I made every effort to clean up the mess because I wanted no one to know that I had attempted to take my own life.

The Headache and The Pit

At 12 years old, I contracted an illness that caused me to have a massive headache. Five people had died in my village already of the same symptoms. It felt like someone was sitting on my brain. It was like drums pounding in my head. My vision was blurry, and I could not swallow. I could only hear the drums. Everything turned dark. The next thing I remember was seeing myself as a four-month-old baby. I was with my grandmother and my stepmother, who had already died. They were arguing over who gets to hold me. It felt like we were in a dark place, like the bottom of a pit. My stepmother held me for a little bit. My grandmother pulled me away from her and said, "She's mine! She's mine!" She started tossing me up in the air playfully and catching me. She tossed me up again, and instead of falling back into her arms, I began to move my arms and legs like I was swimming up in the air. I kept moving myself up until I made it to the top of the pit. I don't know if I was dead or dreaming, but I remember I was with dead people! I escaped from them and, from the top of the pit, peered down and exclaimed, "I will never ever come back again to you!" Suddenly, I turned around as if I was ready to go, and I woke up. My house was filled with people with tears in their eyes. I didn't know if they were crying for me, but as soon as they noticed I was awake, they became quiet for a moment. Then everyone started asking me how I felt and if they could get me anything and started pampering me.

God had a plan for my life. A plan I was unaware of at the time. I could have been dead. What separated me from the people who died? There was no medicine to treat me, but God had a plan for me. And because of that plan, I stand before you today. God has a plan for you, too. Don't lose your hope, and don't give up on yourself because of what you see happening around you. Maybe you're not succeeding in your plans the way you wanted to, but don't give up on yourself! God is not done with you yet!

Chapter 2

When I Met Jesus

When I was 14, I had no pastor or church. I had never even heard the gospel before. I was standing on the third-floor balcony of my home, watching people pass by on the streets. All of a sudden, I heard a loud and audible voice calling my name. The voice said, "*Josephine. Josephine. Do you know who I am? I am the Alpha and Omega. Today is the day of your salvation. I am sending you to go all over the world and preach the gospel. Tell my people I am coming soon.*" There was power in that voice. It shook me to the core. My heart felt like it was being squeezed, and all of the heaviness inside of it was being forced out. My legs, suddenly shaking, gave out, and I collapsed to the floor. I started weeping uncontrollably at the transformation I felt inside. God was moving. When I finally stood up, I felt happy and joyful. A weight had been lifted off me. I felt peace all over me and I was so calm and relaxed, that I headed to my bedroom to sleep.

On the way to my room, I heard a voice inside of me say, "*Don't go to sleep. Go see the woman staying in your house.*" This voice was different from the last. It was not audible; it was like a thought, but not from me. I now know it was the Holy Spirit speaking to me. I went to the kitchen where I found Jackie, our house guest. She had been staying with us for a week, but I was not aware she believed in Jesus. She was reading the story of the crucifixion in the book of Luke. When she read it to me, I burst into tears. I wondered, "How could people do such a thing? What can I do to make him happy?"

Jackie asked, "Do you love Jesus?"

I said, "Of course!"

She led me in the Lord's prayer. I accepted Christ into my heart, and she prayed for me. When she prayed for me, it was like someone shone a flashlight on me, and it illuminated my heart. Words seemed to burst out of my heart in prayer. I prayed for my family, the government, other kids at school, and married couples without even knowing what I was praying for. I told Jackie about my experience hearing the voice on the balcony and the happiness I felt. She listened and believed me.

She said, "I have a place I must take you to tomorrow."

The next day, Jackie took me to a lunch prayer meeting where she introduced me to a group of believers. I was in awe! I found people who spoke in tongues, who were delivered from disease, and who were filled with the Holy Spirit! It was so overwhelming that I only observed from a distance. Dr. Joseph Serwadda spoke during the first meeting. From that day on, he became my pastor. Our house guest and my new friend, Jackie Asiimwe, took me under her wing and taught me how to pray and seek God. Over the next week, we went to meetings together and I met more people who were on fire for Christ. I was fascinated by hearing people speak in tongues and watching demons be cast out of people.

My pastor, Joseph Serwadda, is a firm believer in the Word of God. Hearing him preach the Word of God strengthened me. I felt like I was growing spiritual muscles. As he spoke, my mind would be filled with ideas about how to reach people for Jesus. I wanted to give all of myself to Jesus, but I didn't know how. I didn't feel capable of giving in the way my heart desired. I decided to be an intercessor. Every night, I would go to church and pray. I would intercede from 7 pm to 5:30 am. I'd sleep around 30 minutes at the church and would walk home at 6 am. I was interceding for others instead of sleeping. The church was a two-hour walk from my house. My feet were my only form of transportation. I walked four hours round trip every day. I would be so tired once I got to the church, my body would just want to sleep. But I wouldn't listen to myself. I would remind myself of my purpose for being there. I would not let myself sit down because if I did, I would fall asleep. To motivate myself, I would read the scripture Matthew 6:33,

But seek first the kingdom of God and his righteousness, and all these things will be added to you.

Looking back, I think my diligence in prayer gave me favor with my pastor and his wife. They didn't know that I was praying at the church. No one did. Yet, out of a congregation with a thousand people, the pastor's wife invited me into her home and treated me like family. I felt it gave me the chance to be around them and absorb their wisdom. The pastor asked the young people to start a prayer group that would meet a couple of nights a week! At that prayer group with the young people, we would have so much fun. I prayed like this on a daily basis for three years. I felt like I didn't need anything other than Jesus. I never felt poor or hungry; nothing was as important to me as seeking God.

Chapter 3

When I Was Filled With the Holy Spirit

Iwanted to speak in tongues so badly. I stood at the altar every day asking for tongues. All the believers around me could pray in tongues, but I could not. My church prayed for me but nothing happened. I felt I must not be good enough to speak in tongues.

A few months later, some of the church members drove to Lake Victoria to baptize believers. I believe everyone should have an immersion baptism to fulfill righteousness, just as Jesus was baptized in the Jordan River by John the Baptist in Matthew 3:13. When you are dipped in the water, it's a sign that you are united with Christ and die to your old life. When you are raised from the water, you are also raised to new life and united with Christ through his resurrection. You become a new creation. For me, I was dipped in the lake and when I emerged from the water, I felt a jolt of electricity pulsing through my body. Suddenly, I started speaking in tongues! I felt the fellowship of the Holy Spirit in me. It felt like I was drunk, and two people from the church had to carry me to the shore. I laid down on the sand, praying in tongues. I didn't notice that I was making noise or that my prayers were loud. I just knew that I didn't want to stop. I wish everyone could feel what I felt at that moment. I was changed.

Every Believer Needs the Holy Spirit

What I felt that day was the Holy Spirit. Every person who believes in Jesus needs to be filled with the power of the Holy Spirit. As it says in Romans 8:14 (NIV),

For those who are led by the Spirit of God are the children of God.

John 3 shows how connected the Holy Spirit is to our faith. When Nicodemus asks what it takes to be born again, Jesus replies,

Unless one is born of water and the Spirit, he cannot enter the kingdom of God. (John 3:5)

Like Nicodemus, be born again.

Acts 10 tells the story of Cornelius. Cornelius was a Gentile who was trying to understand what it meant to serve God. God heard Cornelius' prayers. Because of Cornelius' prayers, an angel spoke to Peter about visiting the Gentiles. Peter didn't want to go, and Cornelius didn't know he needed someone to come and talk to him. When Peter spoke to him, life for Cornelius began right there. Cornelius and his whole house were filled with the Holy Spirit.

Why didn't the angel appear to Cornelius and just tell Cornelius everything? Instead, the angel sent Peter to Cornelius. You can see how the body of Christ is meant to function. As believers, it's our assignment to reach out to others through the power of the Holy Spirit.

When you have the Holy Spirit, he will give you gifts. Gifts such as those listed in Galatians 5:22—love, joy, peace, and patience. In Acts 2:4 it talks about the gift of tongues as a gift from the Holy Spirit.

Who Is the Holy Spirit?

The Holy Spirit prepares you. The Holy Spirit prepares the church, who is the bride of Christ, for the groom. In Revelation 22:17, it says,

The Spirit and the Bride say "Come." And let the one who hears say, "Come." And let the one who is thirsty come; let the one who desires take the water of life without price.

When you're led by the Spirit it's easy to connect with God (Romans 8:14). The Holy Spirit shows us how to walk with God and serve him.

The Holy Spirit is gentle. The Holy Spirit does not discriminate against where you come from, the color of your skin, or what you've done as long as you open your heart to Him. In Acts 10, Cornelius, a Gentile centurion, was visited by Peter even though the law forbade Jews from associating with Gentiles. But despite that, the Holy Spirit filled Cornelius and everyone in his home, and they were then baptized in water in the same way the Jews had.

The Holy Spirit is your best friend. The Holy Spirit is a comforter in hard times (Isaiah 40:1). He's your counselor when you need wisdom, and he's the joy when you've lost your peace. He puts a crown on your head when you feel lonely and broken. He raises you up when you're down (Isaiah 61:3).

The Holy Spirit guides you into your future. If we can use technology like GPS to find where we're going and the time we're going to arrive there, then how much more can the Holy Spirit do for us? The Holy Spirit knows everything. He knows what's in the deepest parts of our hearts (1 Corinthians 2:10 and Daniel 2:22). If you're spiritually lost, the Holy Spirit will be your guide. When the Holy Spirit leads you, you walk in the gifts of the Spirit. You are above the law (Galatians 5:18). Your flesh can control you and cause you to mess up, but when you are shaped by the Holy Spirit, you find yourself full of confidence, joy, and love (Galatians 5:22-23).

The Holy Spirit is the power of God. Since Jesus is the Word of life, the Father, Son, and Holy Spirit are one. If you talk about the Holy Spirit, you're talking about the Father and you're talking about the Son as well. If you're talking to Jesus, you're talking to the Father and the Holy Spirit. So if you ask me who the Holy Spirit is, it's the power of God. If you ask me who Jesus is, He's the Word of life. His Word is like bread; you can eat it and live on it (Matthew 4:4). When Jesus walked the earth, he could only travel in one location. But the Holy Spirit covers the whole earth. The Holy Spirit is omnipresent; it doesn't matter if you're in your bed, bathroom, or the church. As long as you call upon the name of Jesus, the power of God will find you (Acts 4:31).

The Holy Spirit is Truth. The Holy Spirit convicts people's hearts. For example, if you've done something wrong, you may forget about it after only a few minutes. Later on, you hear something from deep in your heart, *"Why did you not do good? You need to fix your mistake."* It may be a struggle, but when you come clean, everything is solved. You feel peace and are filled with joy.

The Holy Spirit also helps us bring the truth to our world. There is an enemy telling lies, twisting words, and causing deception. What causes people to speak lies or hide who they really are? The enemy tells people to lie even when they know the truth. The truth is between you and God. When you lie, you give up on yourself and become someone you are not. Be who you are. You know when you're telling lies, and you know when you're telling the truth.

The Healing In My Body

One night, I had a dream. In my dream, someone led me to a staircase that was going down so far that I could not see the bottom. It was very dark at the bottom. Jesus told me," *Everything you see, command it to go to hell in the name of Jesus.*" I looked and saw spirits who took on the form of Indian women wearing saris. They were coming out of my side, one by one. I commanded each one I saw to go in the name of Jesus, and they ran down the stairs and fell into the darkness. I watched 25 of these spirits come out of my side. Once all of them had fallen into darkness, the staircase rolled up like a carpet and vanished.

Jesus said, *"This is your deliverance. Your disease is over. But if you want it back, you can get it again."* Jesus redeemed me that day. I was looking at him, and he was looking at me, and He said, *"Let's go."*

To keep Jesus in my heart, I will live forever free from the spirits. If I deny him, I will receive back the same disease I had just buried. When I woke up, I was looking for Jesus, but he was no longer there. I sat up and felt incredible.

For the first time since I was nine years old, there was no pain in my rib or in my chest. I could walk without pain. I could lift things without pain. Many people had said after the accident with the cow, "You cannot even have kids because of this! Your life is over." But I have been pregnant and had a child just like other women. I was completely healed; I no longer had any pain or injuries. Jesus set me free. Matthew 10:1 says,

> *And he called to his twelve disciples and gave them authority over unclean spirits, to cast them out, and to heal every disease and every affliction.*

If you're seeking healing for your personal life, stand on this Word. God has given you authority over any illness that has been bothering you.

Dr. Serwadda

Dr. Joseph Serwadda is my pastor. He is a man of the Word. Every time he preaches about Jesus, I get a new revelation. He's a humble man. He's a man of action and an evangelist who has led many crusades and has planted many churches. He is the voice of those born again in Uganda. He is a man known for his wisdom. His church prioritizes the Word of God. His goal is to reach souls, and he trains people as well. It was under his ministry that

Dr. Joseph and Frieda Serwadda of Uganda, my spiritual father and mother.

I grew until I started my ministry in Rwanda. He came to Rwanda to ordain me there. He supports me and the whole church. They send people to back me up. Without him, I would not be who I am today. To this day, he is the most special pastor to me. This is a man who would hold a crusade with 150,000 people, but if I called him in the night, he would recognize my voice. He is my spiritual father, and his wife is my spiritual mother. I will never forget the gift they put into my life. They will always remain my spiritual parents.

He led a crusade where many people who were Muslims gave their lives to Christ. It angered the Muslim leaders, and they tried to kill him. They came to a crusade service and opened fire at him. Somehow, the bullets missed him. Three people standing behind him were hit and died. As for him, he was totally fine.

He preached to the Muslims often. His faith challenged them. One time, he was talking to a Sheikh and said, "Tomorrow, you bring your god, and I'll bring my God. We will build a hut for ourselves. We will pour gas on each hut, walk inside the hut, and set it on fire. Then we can see who survives, and that will determine whose God is real."

The next day, Pastor Serwadda showed up with grass, and gas, and was ready to build the hut. The Sheikh never showed up. Up until that day, this Sheikh had been causing confusion in the people and challenging Dr. Serwadda incessantly. The Sheikh never showed up again. Through Dr. Serwadda, I learned about faith.

One time, he was preaching a message at a conference I hosted. He was the keynote speaker. He came down from the stage, pointed to me, and told the ushers to set up a chair for me in front of the stage. He asked the ushers to lift both my right and left hands. He then started preaching in Exodus 17:12, when Aaron and Hur lifted Moses' hands during the battle with the Amalekites.

Dr. Serwada removed his jacket, gave it to me and started talking about me to the people. "This woman, she is not a woman; she is metal. She has a lot in her." Then he said to me, "Listen to me, daughter. I am saying this as a prophet. No one, not even my wife and kids, has received my double anointing. I am giving you my double anointing! The same anointing that is on me to shake the president's hands is on you! I have radio; I prophecy you will have TV. I have traveled around this country, but I see you living overseas! You will have godly people coming around to support you! You will carry the anointing to have many churches."

The team he came with was baffled. They had never seen him talk like this to anyone before. Everyone was looking at me like I was special and had taken the blessing that they were after! The whole evening, the jacket was mine. I went to return it, but he said, "I believe everything God gave you is already in you. Take the jacket." A while later, I eventually gave it back to him.

When this happened, I felt seen by God. Chosen. It was amazing. I love Dr. Joseph Serwadda so much. There are times, even to this day, when I'm seeking confirmation from God, and I will dream about Dr. Joseph Serwadda preaching. Every time I have this dream, his message speaks directly to my situation. I wake up confident in knowing what to do.

After the night he gave me his jacket, I started receiving invitations to travel and minister everywhere. Today, I can say that I have shaken the hands of country leaders, including presidents and a queen. I've traveled to 29 countries all around the world.

Chapter 4

How My Ministry Started

By the time I was fifteen, I was knocking on doors, preaching on the streets, and telling everyone I could about Jesus. I was on fire for God even though I was only a teenager. I could see two spiritual gifts develop in my life. The first was evangelism; I could not pass anyone without sharing Jesus. Sometimes I'd find a way to take the bus so that I could sit and preach to the people. I would stay and preach until the end of the route. The route would start over with a new group of people, and I would preach again!

On other days, I would go to the market and I would pretend like I was crazy! I would clap my hands, sing, and act crazy. People would be surprised and stop to see what's going on. Once I noticed 5-10 people had gathered around me, I would start preaching! People's eyes would be stuck like glue watching me. I would get to the point quickly about Jesus and offer to lead them to Christ. For those who accepted Christ, I would ask them to step to the side, and I would spend time talking with them one on one. Every Sunday, I would bring new people with me to church and introduce them to my pastor, Pastor Serwadda.

During my street evangelism, I was able to raise men and women of God who are now pastoring churches. One of those pastors was my very first disciple for Christ, Frank. Frank was a competitive traditional dancer in Uganda. The other was Joseph, a drummer and an actor. I led Frank to Christ, and then Frank brought Joseph. Both were filled with tons of demonic spirits.

After they were free from spirits, they pleaded, "We don't want to go back to our old lives and be filled with these things again! Do you know what we can do instead of going back?"

I said, "I do! We can serve Jesus using our gifts."

I didn't know how it was going to work but Joseph started writing a song and a musical/play to go with it. He was a very good composer. So Frank, Joseph, and I went to Pastor Joseph Serwadda and explained that we had a musical we wanted to use as a way to reach people. He gave us his blessing and a platform to perform the musical in the church.

People loved it and wanted to join. Over seventy people signed cards saying they wanted to support, so we formed a big choir and started practicing every day. We started looking for big spaces where people gathered, and we could set up our instruments. We also rented out main halls and sold tickets. Hundreds of people would gather. When we started the event, we didn't advertise that we were a church or a Christian organization. If our drama was about wisdom, we would find a song about wisdom, or if it was a drama about family, we would sing songs about family. People would be interested. As soon as the choir stopped, the preacher would preach, and no one would leave. The preacher gave an altar call, the choir would sing worship songs, and we led people to Christ. Everywhere we went, we started new churches. Someone in our group would stay and be the pastor for that location. We would use the money raised from the shows to rent a house for the new pastor and a facility in town to host meetings for the new believers. Pastor Serwadda would provide support by sending members from his church to serve on staff at the churches we planted. When I think about those pastors, it gives me courage to keep ministering. Many of them are very successful pastors now with big ministries.

As that ministry grew, I noticed the second gift in me developing. I started to feel compassion towards people who were tortured and brokenhearted, and a desire grew in me to pray for those people. I just wanted to spend as much time as I could praying for them. The gift of prayer turned into a gift of healing because, as I prayed, they would be healed. I thought, "This is so cool!" I started praying more and more. I could go on my knees all night. I would have overnight prayer nights, worship, and prayer. I didn't need to have the instruments or microphone. I would just use my voice from the bottom of my lungs, and I would shout and yell and pray for everyone and the nation. I don't know what the people saw in me, but eventually, they started bringing their loved ones who were sick. They'd bring their family and friends. Usually, those who were brokenhearted, divorced, or hurting would ask me to pray for them. I picked three days of the week for prayer time. People would come earlier than the start time so they could be the first ones prayed for. There were many miracles. You could see how tortured these people had been.

Chapter 5

The First Miracles

The Woman With a Ghost Boyfriend

We have reason to be upset with the way the devil tortures our world. There was a zeal I would feel when I saw tortured people and prayed for them. Through prayer, I felt I was taking back what the devil had stolen from the kingdom, shooing him away, and commanding him to never come back again. I met this woman who was 50 years old and had been tortured for years and years. When she was a young woman, she had a boyfriend she planned to marry. However, something happened, and they broke up. Later, she decided to become engaged to another man. Her ex, distraught, decided he would take his own life on the day of her wedding. The wedding happened, and the married couple headed to their honeymoon suite. As soon as they got to the room, the ex-boyfriend appeared in ghost form.

The spirit of her ex was jealous and aroused. When she saw him, she became consumed with a desire for him. The spirit moved toward her, and she had sex with him. She felt she had no power to resist. Her husband could not see the spirit but knew his wife was having a sexual experience. She and her actual husband never consummated the marriage that night or any night. The spirit haunted their relationship. She hated every moment. It caused her to lose all desire to be touched by any man, including her husband. She was filled with shame even though she had no desire to be a part of it. Every time she and her husband wanted to get intimate, the spirit would appear. She'd feel an uncontrollable desire for him, but once he was finished with her, she was in so much pain she could not even close her legs or walk. This abuse was constant. The husband was patient and hoped she would be set free and come back to him. However, they both chose to end their marriage. Even after the divorce, she did not get to date anyone else because the ghost ex-boyfriend was too possessive. It was not love; it was torture.

From the ages of seventeen to fifty, she was tortured and miserable. She was haunted by an invisible ex-boyfriend. She didn't know where to hide. She couldn't stop him from visiting her. She wanted to die to escape it. She came to my church group and said, "Woman of God, I don't know what to tell you, but this is my life." As she told me her story, the Holy Spirit opened my eyes so I could see this guy! He was standing near her and waiting for her to finish talking to me so he could take her.

I jumped up and said, "In the name of Jesus, get out of here! By the blood of Jesus, I bind you and command you to leave."

Little by little, he backed away from us until he was outside. Once he was outside, I couldn't see him anymore. I turned to her.

She still saw him and said, "He's standing outside and reaching out to me while telling me I better leave your house and join him."

I started binding the chains that connected them in Jesus' name and told her, "You tell him to leave the compound in the name of Jesus."

She did. He slowly moved back. I told her husband to keep telling him, "Leave in the name of Jesus" and "By the blood of Jesus, I bind you." He moved farther and farther away. Then I told her, "Listen, he has done witchcraft on you, so we need to pray for deliverance." We prayed for deliverance. I invited her to stay for the week so we could continue deliverance. I knew if she went outside, where the ghost ex-boyfriend was, she would not come back.

During deliverance, she started throwing up. She threw up over and over until eventually hair started to come out with the vomit. There was so much hair! It looked like a hairball from a cat. I'd never seen anything like it. After throwing up the hair, she was dizzy and worn out. I let her sleep and gave her water to sip. I read scriptures over her as she napped. I felt like the Holy Spirit said, "Don't leave her now. The battle is still there." In that nap, she had a dream.

She saw the man and told him, "In the name of Jesus! In the name of Jesus!"

He said, "No, don't say that!"

She saw a big white trash bag come from the sky and cover her ghost ex-boyfriend. In her hand appeared an ax! She started attacking him with the ax while he was stuck in the trash bag. She aimed for his neck and swung until his neck was visibly severed from his body, hanging limp. Then a hand appeared and grabbed the bag, closed it, and carried it away. When the hand carried it away, it was over. She felt the anger, pain, unforgiveness, and shame she had held onto her entire life disappear. She woke up. The guy never appeared again. Imagine! She had no freedom from the age of seventeen to fifty, only torture. She enjoyed her new found freedom. Her life began to know Jesus. That's an example of the miracles that took place in the cell group. If God can deliver someone from an invisible horror like this, he can deliver you, too!

The Woman Who Hung From the Ceiling

One of the first miracles I ever saw took place in a home we stopped at when we were out evangelizing. A man opened the door and invited us in. We told him that we were sharing about Jesus. He asked if we could pray for his wife. He walked us into the bedroom where his wife was lying down. She had been sick for three years and was paralyzed in her bed. She was so frail and small that initially, we couldn't tell anyone was in the bed! Together, we lifted her out of the bed, carried her to the living room floor, and propped her up with a pillow so she could sit. We joined our hands, standing around her in a circle. We closed our eyes and prayed for the miracle of her healing. I heard a screech. Alarmed, I opened my eyes, glanced up, and, to my surprise, the woman we were praying for was hanging from the ceiling! It was as if there was a magnet attached to her back, keeping her stuck to the ceiling. Her legs and arms were dangling down.

I screamed, "Look up!."

Everyone looked up and saw her there, and we all started screaming, "In the name of Jesus!"

Immediately, she fell to the floor. We quickly held her down, laid hands on her, and rebuked the devil. We cast out the evil spirits tormenting her. During prayer, we learned why she was suffering from the disease. Her husband's former girlfriend, jealous, sent spirits to kill her. We commanded the spirits to go in the name of Jesus. They left, and she was delivered. This woman, who was paralyzed for three years, was now able to stand in the doorway to see us out and say goodbye. She not only stood up on her own but also took five steps. We were shocked. She was completely healed.

If you're reading this book and you feel like you need freedom, know that freedom is not only available to this woman. Jesus is the only way to receive freedom. In John 14:6 (NIV), Jesus himself said,

> *I am the way, the truth, and the life. No one comes to the Father except through me.*

Your newfound life of freedom can only be found in Jesus.

Power of God

I have seen many things. Sometimes when I am praying for people, I feel the power of God rising inside me. I feel a fire inside of me against the devil. I see the ailment of the person I'm praying for, and I think, "How dare you devil! Doing this to people!" When other people are afraid of the devil, I see the devil the way David saw Goliath! I see him as nothing when Jesus is around! That is my faith.

I think of Peter and John in Acts 3:2-8 who saw a man who was born lame sitting at the gates of the temple. Acts 3:6 (NIV) says,

> *Then Peter said, "Silver or gold I do not have, but what I do have I give you. In the name of Jesus Christ of Nazareth, walk."*

It was the power of God that caused Peter to look into this man's eyes and see the spiritual root of this man's disease. Peter knew he had something to give to this man. The man could not see Peter's gift because what Peter had was invisible. Peter's gift was the words he spoke in the name of Jesus. He knew that what he had was bigger than gold and diamonds. "Such as I have I give thee: In the name of Jesus Christ of

Nazareth." When you say that name, miracles take place. There is no mountain that cannot be moved with the name of Jesus. Your problem may seem like a mountain to you, but when you have the name of Jesus, nothing will stop you from going forward.

When Joshua was preparing to take Jericho in Joshua chapter six, he saw that it was built up with very strong walls, and he didn't know how to enter. Jericho was their "mountain." Even the people of Jericho were intimidating, but Joshua had a word from God. God said to walk around Jericho for seven days, and after seven days, he'd see the miracle. Joshua walked by faith because he had a promise from God. On the seventh day, they walked around the walls and blew their trumpets. The walls cracked and fell down before them. That is what we call the power of God.

Boldness in Approaching God

You won't see the power of God without being connected to God. You have to be serious when talking to God. You must have confidence, knowing deep in your heart and mind that God is real and that whatever you ask for, God will give it to you. With humility in your heart, tell God, "Give this to me, and I will use it to honor You and reach others. This is a deal. You give it to me, and I will give it right back." You must approach God with boldness.

Think of the vow Hannah made in 1 Samuel 1:11 (NIV).

And she made a vow, saying, "Lord Almighty, if you will only look on your servant's misery and remember me, and not forget your servant but give her a son, then I will give him to the Lord for all the days of his life, and no razor will ever be used on his head.

In this verse, Hannah dedicates her firstborn when she was still barren. I'm sure this wasn't the first time Hannah prayed for a child. But this time, she made a pledge. She gave Samuel to God. It says in 1 Samuel 2:21 that after she dedicated Samuel to the temple, God gave her an open womb for even more babies.

Indeed the Lord visited Hannah, and she conceived and bore three sons and two daughters. And the boy Samuel grew in the presence of the Lord.

Be serious about your relationship with God. Treasure it. Don't let it go. Don't be afraid to approach God with boldness. Like Hannah, you will see the power of God.

How I Met My Mother

At the age of sixteen, I decided that I wanted to look for my mother. I was just curious. I wanted to see what she looked like. I wanted to know the woman who gave birth to me. My mother had left us after I was born, and I thought for sure she must be a bad woman for leaving us and not coming back. My older brother and sister knew where she lived, so I went to go see her. When we met, she told me how she had to leave because I was born a girl and not a boy like my father wanted. She tried to come back, but my father's new wife forbade it. A few years later, after my father came to Christ, God spoke to me and told me to take care of my mom. Knowing that inviting my mom to live with me could cause a strain on the relationship between my dad and me, I asked for his blessing first. He gave it willingly. I built a house for her and hired a maid. I led her to Christ. I became her spiritual leader. She grew to become an intercessor. She interceded only for me. She carried a lot of anger against my father for divorcing her and keeping her out of my life until then. It broke my heart to see her so tortured, and I encouraged her to forgive.

My dad and mom eventually apologized to each other. The bitterness between them melted away. There was no more anger. My dad avoided family reunions because my mom was there, and it caused too much tension. Once they forgave each other, my dad joined us for the family reunion. Everyone was amazed at how well they got along. They apologized to my siblings and me for how their treatment of each other affected us. It opened the door for the whole family to follow Jesus. Eventually, the entire family, parents and siblings, chose to follow Jesus. My family was once separated because of my birth, and now my family has reconciled because of my influence on my parents.

The Woman Who Killed and Ate Her Own Children

While praying one night, I heard very clearly from the Lord, "*You're going to Nakaroke,*" and I saw, in my mind's eye, a church building with grass huts in the countryside. I heard, "*This is where you'll go.*" I didn't know anyone there and had no idea how to get there. For a while, I asked everyone I knew if they had heard of a place called Nakaroke or if they had heard of a church in Nakaroke. No one knew. I kept asking everyone I saw.

Two months went by, and then one night at a church group, a new person got up to give a testimony.

He says, "Hey everyone, I'm a guest here. I'm from a faraway place called Nakaroke."

I stopped everything, ran straight to him and gave him a hug. I asked him to tell us about this place. I asked for his contact information, but he didn't have a phone. I asked for an address in Nakaroke to guide me, but he didn't have that either. He did tell me which towns I would pass through to get there. At least it was confirmation that this place existed, but I asked God, "What am I going to do? How will I get there?" God just said, "*Get ready, I'm sending you!*" I fasted for two days, packed my stuff, and headed out towards the direction the guy said.

That journey was a mess! The bus only took us a small part of the way. I had to pay a guy with a bicycle to take me. It was basically all hills, often too steep to bike, so we'd have to walk up. On the way down, it bumped so much and so hard on the bike that I opted to walk. We walked from 3 pm until midnight. By midnight, my feet were covered in blisters. Every step was painful. The bicyclist had enough of the travel. He wanted to go back, especially since he could tell I wasn't sure where I was going. I pleaded with him to stay. He said, "Can't we find a place to sleep?" At that point, we weren't sure where we were or how much further we had to go. When we found someone who would give us a place to sleep, the bicyclist told me he was going to turn back and then left me with them.

By that point, I was in so much pain and so tired. All I wanted to do was rest. I'd try to sleep, but the Holy Spirit wouldn't let me.

The Holy Spirit said to me, "*Are you sure? Are you here to sleep? Go outside and intercede.*"

Out of obedience, I went outside to pray, and oh man, the mosquitos! I grabbed a blanket for protection, but it didn't help. They were everywhere! I persevered and kept praying. I prayed until 6 am. I went back inside to sleep, but by that point, everyone was waking up. The people who hosted me noticed me and asked me to join them for breakfast. As they prepared breakfast, I took a walk to keep myself awake. In front of me, I saw a very familiar-looking church building. "Hmmm, what is this?" I thought to myself. Then the Lord brought to my mind the vision he gave me of the church in Nakaroke, and I realized I was here! I actually made it to Nakaroke! I started praising God and got on my knees to thank Him.

While praying, I suddenly felt the hairs on the back of my neck stand up. I looked behind me and saw a woman headed in the direction of the church. Walking next to her was a giant Spirit that looked like a bodyguard. I didn't know what to do, so I just stood in place and started speaking in tongues. As I was doing that, and I was speaking very loudly, the people who let me stay at their house came out to offer me tea. They heard me praying intensely and told me that they were pastors! It was at that point the woman with the bodyguard spirit noticed me.

She started screaming, "You! You! Why are you here?" Then she started charging right at me! I asked two guys nearby to grab her and hold her back. They tried, but she was too strong. Two more guys came, and even the four of them could not hold her down. She kicked at everything to get away–the walls, the bench, anyone that came close. She was fighting back so hard that her thigh started bleeding from the struggle, but it was like she didn't even notice.

It took seven men to finally hold her down. I told them to tie her down to something first, and then we would bandage up the bleeding. After she was restrained, we prayed and prayed. Two hours went by, and the spirits wouldn't leave. I kept asking God, "What is this spirit, and what is going on here?" I would command it to leave. It would pretend to leave, but I could see it was still there. They argued that they deserved to stay because they made a covenant with this woman. We learned that this woman had sacrificed two of her babies to the devil. We were shocked. When it comes to deliverance, it's important not to try and argue with demons. Respond to them only with scriptures.

A woman from the town came to see what was going on. It turns out she also was tormented by spirits and started to act violently just like the other woman! The men had to restrain her as well. So now there were two women tied on the floor, demon-possessed!

The spirits in the first woman turned to the other woman next to her and said, "Thank you for coming! Let's make them work until their energy is drained. She will become too tired to cast us out."

It was like a light bulb went off in my mind when I heard that, and I realized God just exposed their strategy to me. The demons wanted to wait me out, to exhaust me, but I knew that wasn't their decision to make!

 I turned to the people with me and said, "We have prayed and cast these demons out in Jesus' name. They have no authority; they must submit to the name of Jesus and leave. It's done. Let's go have tea."

The people with me disagreed. They saw the women, still tied to the floor, writhing and possessed, and argued, "How can we leave when the women are still like this? We need to keep praying!"

I said firmly, "No. We leave now to drink tea and eat breakfast. Our prayer has done the work. These women are free."

We left and sat to drink tea and eat breakfast. As we ate, we heard yelling from the area where we left the women, "AHHH! They are ignoring us! We have to go! We have to go! Ahh! The burning! This fire! This fire! Don't kill us; we're leaving right now!" And then it got quiet. We returned to the women and found them sitting, wondering what had happened to them. We untied them. It's clear to me now that when we left the room to eat breakfast, Jesus took control and set those women free.

Now that the women were free, the first woman with the giant spirit told us her story. For a long time, she heard many voices. Voices that tortured her and directed her to do horrible things. When she was married to her first husband and was a new mom, these voices told her, "Get your baby and put him in the fire." She did it. She put her own baby in the fire and then started eating him. She was horrified when she returned to her senses and realized what she had done. She couldn't look her husband in the eye. She couldn't live with herself, so she ran away, far enough that no one could find her again. Eventually, she remarried and became pregnant again. The same thing happened again with the second baby. By the time she arrived in Nakaroke, she was so distraught, and the voices were telling her to throw herself into the lake to drown. When she saw me, she was headed to the lake to do just that.

After the women were delivered, we were asked to hold a conference at the church. We were there for a week hosting services. Every day, more and more people would come. The whole village had heard the story and came out to see for themselves. The women were now a part of the church and were the example of God's power. That woman's testimony brought many people to Christ. At the end of the week, the church was packed with new converts.

Chapter 6

The Betrayal in the Church Group

In six months, our church's cell group grew very quickly from just a few people to around eighty people who would meet consistently with me. They'd fill my house, and when there was no more room, they'd sit outside in the compound. They'd bring an extra piece of clothing and lay it out on the ground like a blanket to sit on. This went on for months, and eventually, we had to move to another person's house that could accommodate the number of people. After around five months, I was invited to evangelize in a village in the countryside. This countryside village didn't have electricity, so it was pitch black. That night, as I was preparing to go to sleep, I heard, "*Josephine, sit down, let me show you something.*" I clearly heard it as if someone was in the room with me. A picture of a television appeared on the wall before me. A voice said, "*I am going to show you what is taking place in your cell group.*"

On the television, I saw these people who I thought were my best friends and good people. They were the leaders I left in charge of the cell group while I went to this countryside village to preach. I saw around five people sitting together on the TV, and I could hear their words. They were talking about me. "She cannot be a leader. She's a child! Who wants to be led by a kid?" They decided that I would not be allowed to preach when I came back. They even said when she returns, this is how we are going to treat her. Whoever is holding the meeting, carry on. Don't introduce her. Don't even mention her. Just keep preaching. Then, right before you close the service and everyone is already starting to leave, say, "Oh! Josephine is here! Let's invite her to do a greeting." That way the service would basically be over and no one would stay. When I heard that and saw it on the TV, it broke my heart. I felt nauseous from the betrayal of my friends. The TV disappeared.

God said, "*Be prepared, and when you go back, don't stir up a fight.*"

When I arrived back at my house, it was the day of the cell group meeting, but I stayed home. Around the time the service would be ending, I heard the Lord tell me, "*Go, stay for four minutes, sit in the back, and don't talk to anyone.*" I went, and I could tell the leaders started panicking. They thought I'd jump in and say something. They were sweating and looked concerned. But after four minutes, the Holy Spirit told me it was time to leave, and I walked out. The Holy Spirit told me to go again the next day, but only visit in the last ten minutes. I sat even farther in the back and stayed for only ten minutes. I didn't talk to anyone, and I walked out. The third night, I left after five minutes. I didn't even give them the chance to welcome me. I heard the Holy Spirit say, "*This is the last day; you won't come back here. It's over.*" I never returned, but I heard the church had dissolved after only a few months. When I got home, I had a dream about going to Rwanda.

Chapter 7

Visiting Rwanda

In December 1994, I had a dream. In it, I stood in front of a big, lush field full of all kinds of trees and fruits. God said, *"This is the field I have prepared for you. You need to go back to your home country."* Before that, Rwanda wasn't in my heart. Initially, I was excited to reunite with the family members we left behind, but nothing was as I expected when I arrived. It looked like the devil visited my country. The streets were filled with corpses. Homes and rivers were, too. Everywhere you turned, bodies were lying around. Even the Catholic church in town was filled with dead bodies. I learned that the priests betrayed their own people. They invited people to come inside for protection. However, they were actually setting them up to be killed. Women killed women. Best friends turned against one another. Kids were trained to kill other kids. They killed each other with machetes and knives. It was like the whole country had been brainwashed.

I remember seeing a woman whose skull had been severed, her brain hanging out the side. It wasn't just the people. Even the dogs were trained to be predators. They would chew on dead bodies and roam the streets with human limbs hanging from their mouths.

Even though the genocide had officially ended by that time, there was still rampant killing going on. It was not safe to walk outside. In my three days there, I walked around to see what the country looked like. I crossed the street, and I heard two soldiers arguing.

One says, "Do it now!" And the other says, " I can't do it."

I heard their guns cocking, and I saw people running and finding a place to hide away from the street. I huddled in with a group for safety. The next thing I knew, one of the soldiers fired their gun and hit the man next to me! The bullet hit his throat, and blood was gushing everywhere. When I saw him, I knew he was as good as dead.

I jumped immediately over to him, looked him in the eye, and said, "Do you know Jesus? If you don't, you don't have any time, repeat this prayer with me."

He attempted to pray as best he could. After the prayer, his eyelids started to droop as he began to lose consciousness. By this time, everyone else had run away, and I had to run for my life.

Finding My Family

The dogs, bodies, and the experience of seeing this man die in front of me was too much. I wanted to turn around and go back to Uganda because the devastation was so bad. But before I did, I wanted to find my family that had stayed in Rwanda. I discovered there was not a single family member in Rwanda left. All of my uncles, aunts, cousins, and even my brothers who had come back to rescue them were all killed. In total, I lost twenty people in my family. Every single one was forced into the same grave and buried alive.

I thought I better head back. I bought a ticket back to Uganda. I hopped on the bus and heard God's voice speaking to me as I sat in my seat. I heard, "*Josephine. Are you running away from your calling? I sent you to help your own people. Are you running like Jonah?*" I started weeping. I wept and wept. I had no money; I spent it all to return to Uganda. I wept and pleaded with the Lord to have mercy on me and let me stay in Uganda. I was so confused. I wanted to leave Rwanda so badly, but I also wanted to obey the Lord. Finally, I said, "Lord, let me go back to Uganda, pack all my stuff, and then come back to Rwanda for good." And that's what I did. I packed my stuff and returned to Rwanda like I promised the Lord.

Chapter 8

The Orphanage

When I returned to Rwanda, orphans were everywhere. One evening in prayer, God said, "*Josephine, take care of the orphans. Be their mother.*" God then showed me the face of a person to look for and told me his name was Eugene, and he owned a house for orphans. Later that week, I saw the same man God had shown me in the vision. I asked if I could bring the orphans I knew to his orphanage. He agreed.

Despite asking if I could bring my kids, I didn't know what kids I was referring to. At the time, I hadn't met any orphans who wanted to be in my care! As I was walking home, I passed through the market. A bunch of kids called out, "Mama! Mama!" and they started running to me as if they knew me!

They surrounded me and cried, "Mama, take me with you. Boss, please take me home with you! I am tired of being on these streets! I'll be good to you. I'll serve you!"

They showed me bruises on their arms, and the bullet fragments still lodged in their heads. Their skin was covered with rashes. They smelled terrible, but the amazing part was how they flocked to me that day. Each of them starts telling me their own story to win my favor so I'll take them home. These kids didn't have anyone left for them. Before I picked them up, they were sleeping in the boxes on the street. When the rain would come, they had nowhere to go. They would stand in the rain until it was gone.

I brought fifty kids back to Eugene's orphanage with me. When he saw me, he was stunned! He thought I meant one or two. He didn't expect me to bring fifty! We agreed that I would take care of the kids, including the ten already there. I became a mama. I treated them all equally and showed them love. Caring for those kids was a calling on my life during my time there.

Being a Mother to Orphans

I knew this calling was to keep the kids off the streets and train them to be God's army—to teach them the Word of God, to pray for them, and to teach them good behavior. God helped me, and it worked very well. Each night, we would have evening service together and worship God. I would share the word of God, and they would burst into tears and cry and cry and cry in repentance. As they wept, they looked like young adults, not little children. I would cry as well, not knowing why they were crying, until one by one, I'd hear them confess through their tears, "Jesus, I'm sorry I killed my friend(s). I'm so sorry! I hope you can forgive me." I couldn't believe what I heard! These kids God gave me to raise were the same kids who were involved in killing during the genocide. They were trained to kill other kids. I started talking to them one by one about their experience, which was the beginning of healing for them. Every time they would confess, I would pray for them and give them scriptures to comfort them. I did that with all of them until I knew each of them and their histories— how their parents taught them to kill, how many kids they killed, how they felt when they were killing, how they felt after, how they feel now, etc. We talked through all of that. They would repent and weep for three hours at a time.

After hours of seeking God, I sometimes asked, "Why are you crying so much?"

They'd respond, "Jesus is so strong in me!"

I learned a lot while serving those kids. Because those kids were trained to kill other kids during the genocide, God desired to bring them to repentance. They all repented and were baptized in water and the Holy Spirit.

Many people warned me to stop what I was doing because it wasn't healthy for me. They'd tell me that these kids, who had killed many people, would one day kill me. My family avoided me because they did not think it was a good idea.

I have learned through life experiences that many people if they don't hear from God and blindly accept the counsel of others, may end up losing what God has for them. God tells you clearly to do something. In that moment, you know in your heart that God is giving you that direction. But you question what God said when you walk outside or go home. You ask your friends what they think. This can be dangerous. If I had listened to my family, it would have made me run from the calling of God. I decided not to focus on what they said, but I decided if those kids decided to take my life, I was ready to die for them.

God's Provision to the Orphanage

In the orphanage, we didn't have money or food. No farm to grow food. No bank account to store or withdraw funds. There was not much support from anyone locally. The beginning was very hard. Sixty kids is not a small number; the youngest was only six months old. At only sixteen years old, I was still just a kid myself. I prayed that God would provide food, blankets, sheets, and clothing to care for these precious children. Every time I prayed, God would tell me where to go and who to talk to. He would give me specific names. That was the foundation of our orphanage and a foundation to have more faith in God. Sometimes during prayer, God would give me the name of an organization such as the Good Samaritan, UNICEF, or the UN, and He would tell me exactly where it was located and how to get there. Knowing how to get there was a critical piece because we didn't have GPS or phones; I only had the voice of God!

One day a Danish visitor came with Pastor Serwadda from Uganda. The visitor asked, "How do you feed these kids?"

I said, "We don't have a farm to feed kids, and we don't have a way to get these kids food!"

He questioned again, "So how do you feed them?"

I said, "Since you ask so much, I will show you." I took him to our storage room/pantry. It was completely empty. I got on my knees and cried out, "Food! I command you! Come now, in the name of Jesus! The kids are hungry! Food! In Jesus's name, I command you to come right now! Amen!" Then I stood up and said, "It's done. The food is on the way."

Miracle service in Denmark. A lady was healed and walked for the first time in 8 years after being paralyzed by cancer.

He was bewildered. He started laughing. He said, "Have you sent someone to go to the market to get the food?"

I said, "No."

He said, "It's good that you pray, but the kids need to eat tomorrow. You don't have food for them."

I said, "It's done! We prayed, and the food will come."

Before it was time for him to leave for the day, we heard the sounds of vehicles approaching—first one truck, then two! Trucks full of food, flour, sugar, cooking oil, beans, and even bedsheets! No one knew this truck was coming! It was not on the schedule. Kastin, the Danish visitor, was AMAZED.

He said, "This is real faith."

He started calling his friends in Denmark to tell them they must come and see for themselves.

This kind of situation happened many times. Sometimes, we would have no food, and I would tell all the cooks to wash the pots and pans and to prepare the table even though there was nothing to eat. We would tell the kids to wash their hands to get ready to eat. Then I would look to God and say, "We've done our part; now it's your part to bring the food." And every time, God would provide. Whether it was a visitor with gallons of milk or pieces of cake, it always happened. God is so good.

God helped me start with nothing. As the Scriptures say in Hebrews 11:6,

And without faith it is impossible to please him, for whoever would draw near to God must believe that he exists and that

he rewards those who seek him.

It takes faith to believe God is there, and He is listening to you. No matter what it is, God listens and responds to our faith.

Chapter 9

My First Church

Through those kids, revival took place. Every evening, we had an evening of glory with fellowship and prayer. The kids would pray for three hours non-stop. Then, we would share the Word. The people in the neighborhood would hear the worship and come and give their lives to Christ just by seeing how God used those children in prayer. Through these kids, God said to me, "You've been faithful to the little. I want to give you a big assignment." God told me that he wanted me to be a shepherd to adults. After that, the kids and I traveled from house to house, ministering and preaching the gospel of Jesus. Many people gave their lives to Christ, and eventually, we had 120 people joining us weekly for worship. That was the beginning of the Rwanda Victory Mission.

Beaten By My Team Members

For us, 120 people was a big number. Because of the growth, I knew I needed a team to help me, but the people I was training found it extremely hard to believe that a woman could lead a church. At that time in Rwanda, women were not pastors. Women were active in the church by singing in the choir, ushering, or being pastors' wives, but not as leaders. Some of the men in my church were embarrassed to be under a woman's leadership. They thought it was more appropriate for me to give up my role as pastor to one of the men. One Sunday, I went to church as usual. During the service, five of my fellow brothers in Christ, men that I was building up to be church leaders, grabbed me in front of the entire congregation and started cursing me.

They said, "How dare you, a woman, stand up and preach while there are men sitting down! Don't you feel ashamed?"

They closed in on me to beat me. There was no time to ask for help. They tossed me around between them like a ball. They did it in front of everyone. Not one person came to my rescue. While they beat me, one of the men started preaching. At that point, they released me from their arms. Furious, I decided that I needed to help myself. I wanted to hit one of the men standing in front of me. As I reached to grab a bench, I heard the Holy Spirit say, "*Don't break what you have started to build. Go sit down.*" After I heard that voice, I went to sit down broken-hearted. The pain of the betrayal was beyond anything I can describe. After a moment, I felt like I needed to go home, so I gathered my belongings and left without saying goodbye to anyone.

When I got home, I burst into tears with the level of grief of someone who had lost a loved one. I screamed. I cried aloud and let all of the anger come out of me. "God why!! Why did you let this happen? Why did you let me work so hard to build a church for it to be taken from me? Why did you let me get beat in front of my whole church?" No response. The next day, silence. I thought God would at least come and apologize for what happened, but he didn't show up. He didn't say He was sorry or anything. I swore that I would never preach again. I didn't leave the house. I was really upset and frustrated. I didn't know what to do.

On the third day, I heard Jesus say, "*Josephine, I want you to bless the men who beat you. Bless them three times every day—once in the morning at 6 am, once at noon, and again at 6 pm. Do it for two years and never curse them.*" I obeyed, but not without difficulty. Most days, I did it through tears. If you were to look at me from the outside, you'd see my tears while praying and think the Holy Spirit moved me, but I was not! I was crying because I was so hurt, broken, and angry by the betrayal. I didn't want to bless them; I wanted to pay them back! My heart said one thing, but the Holy Spirit said another. What I didn't realize is that blessing them would turn into medicine for myself. I was healed from the pain of that incident by praying for them. I blessed them three times daily, for two years straight. As for my church, I never went back. They never apologized, and I never said anything to defend myself about what happened. I just disappeared. That was the end of my first church.

Sermon On Forgiveness

Forgiveness starts in your house, in your family, and in your community. Before we ask for forgiveness from God, he wants us to reconcile with our neighbor. Matthew 5:23-24 says,

> *So if you are offering your gift at the altar and there remember that your brother has something against you, leave your gift there before the altar and go. First be reconciled to your brother, and then come and offer your gift.*

When you go before God, if anyone caused you to stumble, seek reconciliation before you go to God. Scripture says when you forgive, you will be forgiven. Matthew 6:14 says,

> *For if you forgive others for their transgressions, your heavenly Father will also forgive you.*

Psalm 86:5 says,

> *For you, O Lord, are good and forgiving, abounding in steadfast love to all who call upon you.*

When you forgive, you change. Your heart starts to shine. It is filled with love. Forgiveness helps you love your enemies and heal from wounds. If you choose to carry anger, it only creates confusion. Every time you see a person or someone who hurts you, it frustrates you. Keeping your peace is hard, so forgiveness is important in our lives.

Another Betrayal

Within a few months, God instructed me to start a lunch-hour meeting at the orphanage. Instead of eating food, people would leave

Preaching in Rwanda at my first church.

work to come to eat the Word! I preached on reconciliation, the power of miracles, and how God can help them. The people needed to hear about reconciliation after being tortured by genocide. They were living in a state of trauma. The whole country was traumatized because everyone had lost family members. The rumors spread around town about the miracles happening during those lunch meetings. I became known for praying for people. They would bring their friends who had been traumatized from the genocide and could no longer function. HIV was spreading rapidly across the country as well. I remember three people who were healed from HIV during those meetings. People would come bedridden and leave completely healed and restored by God. The meeting grew in attendance quickly because the capital city was talking about the revival taking place.

The men who had beaten me became very jealous of what was happening. They thought they had already dealt with me. This made them furious to the point where they wanted to take my life. Their first plan was to ambush me on my route to the orphanage. They would place themselves on my route so that when I passed, they could jump me. Each time, I would have a dream the night before where I would see the faces of these men standing in my route, waiting for me with stones in their hands. Then, in my dream, I'd hear a voice say, *"Don't go that way."* I would wake up the next day and send someone to look to check. Sure enough, the person would return, describing the men standing exactly where the Holy Spirit had revealed to me.

Frustrated, the men then became allies with another church. They asked the other church to help stop me. If they did, the church would submit to their leadership. Now, I had two churches coming after me! One day, members from both churches came to my meeting as a large group determined to hijack my service. They created confusion and chaos in the room. Every time I tried to preach, they drowned out my voice with their own. They mocked me. They screamed over me, yelling accusations and calling me a liar. We didn't have a stage or a sound system to show who was leading the service. The members didn't understand what was going on and were confused. Most of them were new Christians who were just coming for healing. I was outnumbered. I left my service with a broken heart.

Preaching on the radio in Rwanda.

That night, I cried to God. I asked, "Why did you make me a minister, if you can't protect me? I need to make a case for myself to report those people." The country was still hurting from genocide. During the genocide, the churches betrayed the citizens and aided the killers by luring people into the church and then handing the keys to the building over to the killers. So I knew winning my case as a minister would be tough. Even still, I decided to report them and wrote up the case. That night, I had a dream. Jesus appeared and told me to cancel the plans to go to the court. He told me this was His battle and to burn the papers. When I woke up, I burned the case I wrote against those men. Even still, I was frustrated. The first time when I was beaten, Jesus just told me to pray for them and forgive them. I couldn't even curse them. Now I found myself betrayed a second time, and I couldn't even defend myself by bringing my case to court. I felt like God doesn't care about me. He must love the people who betrayed me more.

Pain From The Betrayal

I felt a pain in my heart that I had never experienced before. When I lost my family in the genocide, it hurt. But this pain of being persecuted, of being tortured, and of being kicked out would eat at me. It was horrible. I was upset with God. I didn't say I was upset. I just hid it in my heart and planned that as soon as possible, I would go back to Uganda. In the meantime, I never left my house. I hid from everyone. I didn't see the kids; I didn't go to church. I felt like there was nothing left for me. I felt defeated.

One Sunday, as I was getting ready to leave the country and never come back, I heard a knock on my door. Guess who's there? Three of the new Christians that I left at the first church!

They exclaimed, "Hey, pastor! We're here! Finally, we found you!"

I was hesitant. I didn't want to open the door for them, but they said they searched everywhere for me.

They had, in their hands, the Bibles I gave them and said, "What are we going to do with these Bibles without you? If you don't teach us, we will have to give them back."

I told them to wait, and I went to my bedroom. I said to the Lord, "I told you I wasn't going to preach anymore! Send them away, Lord!" I left them on their own for thirty minutes hoping they would leave. I told myself I wouldn't preach again because the more I preach, the more I give myself trouble. They wouldn't leave. Eventually, I thought they are my guests, so I might as well pray for them and then send them away. I said, "God, if you have one scripture, I will read it, but that's it. I won't explain it." God gave me a scripture. I started reading, and when I did, the anointing of God fell upon my house, and it was so strong!

I started preaching and preaching. The spiritual babies were baptized by the Holy Spirit and lying on the floor, tears streaming down their faces. Then, they started laughing in the spirit, prophesying, and crying. It went on the whole day! We started around 9 am and finished around 9 pm. NONSTOP prayer, can you believe it??! By the afternoon, I was panicking. I wanted them to stop, get something to eat, drink, and use the restroom, but they were so drunk in the spirit they wouldn't move. I was concerned for their health! I raised my voice to tell them to stop, but they wouldn't listen. I started repenting to God, "I beg you to forgive my sins. God, I'll do whatever you want as long as you let them walk home in freedom." I went to them, and they managed to get up. They prophesied, "Pastor, we see you're going far away from this country. You are a woman of faith and will plant many churches."

Chapter 10

A Church of My Own

Everyone went home, and I had a dream that night. In it, God showed me where to start a new church. It was a broken house with no windows. I was concerned about being betrayed again, but God said, "*Don't worry. It is over. You have passed the test. No one shall stand before you. You shall build the church, and no gates of hell will break it again.*"

My friend, you could be in a similar situation or feeling the same kind of pain that I felt. You may feel betrayed or like you have nowhere to go. You may feel like no one listens to you. Jeremiah 29:11 (NIV) says,

> *For I know the plans I have for you," declares the Lord, "plans to prosper you and not to harm you, plans to give you hope and a future.*

God has a plan for you. If you feel the way I did, I can assure you that God will rescue you in the same way he did for me. He reminded me that I could not run away from my calling. I will stay, and I will serve. After that day, everything was clear and clean in my heart. I started over again. There was no more battle in my heart. God brought me to the building he showed me in the dream, and we started a new church.

The Retaliation from the Muslim Witch Doctors

We stayed at the house without windows for four years in total peace. I was able to minister without trouble the entire time we stayed there. After those four years, God showed me a new place to buy land and build a church. This land was previously owned by Muslims who had wanted to use it to build a mosque but were in debt and decided instead to sell. The owners were not aware that they were selling to a Christian. The members of the church began cutting down trees and clearing the land. The owners asked what we were doing with the land, and we told them we were building a church. The owners began panicking when they realized what they had done. They fought to obtain the land. They started doing voodoo and witchcraft to destroy our efforts to build the church. However, they had no power to stop it. The church was built, and more and more people attended.

High-ranking Muslim leaders from Dubai, India, Libya, Nigeria, and Rwanda decided to gather to put an end to our mission. They believed they would curse me until I dropped dead. During the cursing time, the ritual to kill me was to sit in a circle and put a bucket of water in the center of the circle. One person stood at the top of the bucket filled with water with a dagger, and they would all call my name. Typically, during this ritual, the face of the person whose name was called would appear in the water. Then the witch doctor would take the dagger and stab the water where the face appeared, and the person, wherever they were in the world, would die instantly.

The witch doctor stood over the bucket for seven days, calling my name and waiting for my face to appear. Instead of my face appearing, something else happened. The bucket of water burst! Water ran everywhere! Everyone sitting there jumped up and ran for their life! They had never seen this happen before and knew it was from something greater than their powers. They began screaming that I was a witch and ran for their lives! They feared that if the water from the bucket touched them then they would be the ones to die.

"I Will Bring Her Heart to You"

One of the female Muslim witch doctors told everyone that she would go and finish it herself. She would bring my heart to them, still beating in her hands. On a Sunday morning, she approached the church to take my life. As she came to enter the building, I felt something in my spirit that spiritual warfare was going on and needed prayer. I stopped the sermon and told everyone to stand up and pray. I instructed the congregation to speak in tongues, bind evil spirits, and seal themselves with Jesus's blood. Before she could take another step, she dropped dead.

Church security spotted her and started screaming, "Someone is dead behind the church!"

Everyone was scared, but I told them there was nothing to fear. I said, "Let me say a prayer of dismissal for the service. You all can go home, and we will deal with it." Everyone was dismissed and the ushers brought her body inside the church for me to pray for her. We started praying. Her body started smelling as if she had been dead for an entire week. The smell was so strong. I stayed and prayed, and God revealed to me that spirits had killed her. I started rebuking demons of death. I told her to return to life now. She opened her eyes.

She said, "Wow, they're looking at me."

I said, "Who?" She replied, "They are!" By "they," she meant the faces of the demons tormenting her.

She said, "They are telling me to leave with them! If I don't leave, they say they will kill me."

I said, "There is no death here in the name of Jesus. Don't leave, stay."

She stayed. I led her to Christ, and she was delivered from the spirits. She told me about the other witch doctors and the bucket, how they all ran for their lives when it busted, and her plot to destroy me.

When She Gave Birth to a Tumor

The woman stated she could not go back to the Muslim religious leaders because they would kill her. I decided to take care of her. I found her a home and hired people to protect her. The battle shifted from me to her. Those religious leaders sent many forces to kill the woman. I started taking care of her and taught her to seek Jesus. Soon after, she got cancer in her stomach. A tumor grew in her belly. As I prayed for her, the Lord revealed to me that she was cursed and the tumor was an attack. That night, she had a dream that she was in a hospital gown, and I was in a doctor's uniform, helping her to give birth. She woke up in crazy pain. She felt sharp, labor-like pains. She grabbed a bucket nearby and started to push. She kept pushing until a 6 pound tumor came out of her body. She put it in the bucket as a way to save it for me to see since she knew I visited every morning and evening. As usual, I dropped by the following day. She showed me the tumor sitting in the bucket. It was so gross; the sight made me puke. I didn't want to discourage her; I wanted to give her the opportunity to get rid of it. We buried it and cast out any more devils of cancer. She was delivered. I anointed her, we took communion, and she was free. A month later, we started organizing crusades together. She was ready and open to testify against the witch doctors in her preaching. She grew stronger, and everywhere we would go to preach, the local leaders would bring cops to protect her because she angered the witch doctors because of her testimonies.

Chapter 11

Miracles in Rwanda

Crippled Man Who Made A Secret Covenant

A man from the military got really sick to the point where the military decided to send him back to his family. He had a hunched back; he could not stand alone or walk. Due to the disease, the military discharged him. They dropped him off at his house. He managed to crawl from his home to the church compound next door. The church was fasting that week. During a week of fasting, people come to the church at all hours in shifts to pray. I directed everybody to go to varying corners of the compound to pray.

As everybody was praying, one of the church members yelled to me, "Pastor! Can you come help me here?" I go over, and I see my church member standing near a crippled man who was skinny and frail. I look at this frail man and ask his name and where he's from. As we talked, I felt a lot of compassion for him and needed to help him. I asked the team to lift him and carry him inside the church. We started to pray for him. Each time we prayed, little changes in his body would show that the prayer was working. I decided to keep the intercessors and him there at the church for continued prayer. We brought him a mat to sleep on, and his family brought food. Little by little, we watched his back straighten, and his limbs stretch out. People would pray until they got tired, and another team would take over. After one week, he improved so much that he could stand straight and walk normally. He accepted Jesus in his heart and started serving in the church.

We thought the healing was complete, but there was a secret.

Sometimes, people, in an effort to seek help for themselves, make covenants with forces without realizing the impact of their choices. They don't realize that they are, in effect, digging their own grave and doing themselves more spiritual harm than good. Seven months later, as I was preaching during a church service, I turned around and said to Edward, "You! You need to come to overnight prayer because God wants to help you and deliver you from something you've never shared with us." He came to prayer, and we started worshiping. Edward fell to the ground as we worshiped, almost like he was in a trance. He lay very still with his eyes closed, but he was breathing. The church prayed in tongues. We knew this was a manifestation of demons and asked Jesus to deliver him. An hour went by and nothing happened. The demons wouldn't leave. We prayed all the prayers we knew. Bewildered, I asked Jesus, "Jesus, I've never seen anything like this before. What kind of spirit is this? Help me understand."

I nearly gave up when Jesus revealed the problem to me. He showed me that Edward had made a blood covenant with the devil. Edward promised that he would give his heart to the devil for the rest of his life. I walked up to Edward and said, "Devil, you cannot hold his heart anymore." This man, who had been lying perfectly still for an hour, started screaming and looking at me with contempt. I started praying for Edward to retrieve consciousness and for the devil not to manifest so he could tell me about the covenant and break it. Edward managed to come out of the trance and sit up. He confirmed to me that he had visited the witch doctor and had nicked himself near his heart to give blood. He made a blood covenant. It was a covenant that signified that the witch doctors could do whatever they wanted to his life. When he was lying motionless on the ground, he told us he could see the same witch doctor and was surrounded by those demonic forces telling him, "You cannot denounce it. You made a covenant with us. You cannot change it." The devil was confusing him not to change it.

When it comes to covenants, blood is involved, but the words are the real covenant. We can easily say things, but those words can become a rope around your neck. Be careful about what you say. Proverbs 18:21 says,

*Death and life are in the power of the tongue, and those who
love it will eat its fruit.*

When I asked him who he made a covenant with, he remembered
the witch doctor. I asked him to remember the exact words he shared.
Based on what he said, I told him what to write and how to pray about it
and told him to talk to the witch doctors as if they were there. He called
them out by name and renounced them in the name of Jesus. He said,
"It's over! I'm no longer your servant. I dedicate my life to Jesus." Then
we prayed for him, and he started manifesting again.

As we prayed this time, we learned that the demons had claimed his
seed. Again, I commanded the demons to stop manifesting and Edward
to wake up. He comes back and confesses that nothing reproductive
works, and he figured he would never be able to have kids or a wife. I
said, "Stop it. You will have kids and a wife. This has no more power
over you." We kept praying and declaring that these demons had no more
control over his body. We taught him to pray over himself, to claim his
seed back, and to walk in faith. He spent the next month at the church,
seeking God. Soon after, he became the security guard for our church.
Little by little, he started feeling more like himself and felt like he was
normal.

One day, he asked me, "Can I marry?" I said let's pray and ask
God if you can marry. We did, and God said yes, so I told him he could
marry. His whole family was against it. They were sure it would end in
divorce due to reproductive issues. He fell in love, married, and had five
kids with his wife! The whole town knows him as a man with integrity
because of his love for Jesus. The military even wanted him back because
they saw he was back to normal, but he said no. He was a completely
changed and healed man.

For those of you reading, you may believe things in your life cannot
be moved or changed. I'm telling you that God moves mountains! Just
put any problem you have at Jesus's feet, and he will take care of it.

Father Led to Christ

When I was eighteen years old, my father gave his life to Christ.
While sowing into other families, I believed that God would reap a

harvest in my family as well. My father was a very tough person. He was Catholic and did not like my faith. There was a constant battle between us. At some point, he fell sick. He was hospitalized, and the doctors stated that nothing could be done for him. They discharged him and told him to go home to die.

As everyone awaited his death, my father had a vision. He saw an angel with a huge sword enter through the ceiling of his bedroom. He was so shocked he fell from his bed! He started screaming, "Don't kill me! I beg you! I'll do whatever you want." The angel told him that he needed to repent for his evil work and for rejecting me as his daughter. He was told to go and look for me. He got on a bus immediately and traveled the whole night to see me. At 10 am the next day, I heard a knock on my door. I opened the door to find my father standing before me.

He was crying, "Give me Jesus. Give me Jesus before I die."

Confused, I asked, "What are you talking about?"

Once again, he said, "Give me Jesus."

I thought that he was tricking me. I knew my father as the one who fought me concerning my faith. Finally, I relented and led him through the salvation prayer. My father confessed his sins and was reconciled with the Lord as His savior.

When he arose from his knees, he asked me for one favor, "Would you please find room in your heart to forgive me? Would you please let me be your spiritual son, and you be my spiritual mother?"

We forgave one another, and from that moment, a new life began for us. When my father returned to his home, he called his family together. He said, "If you live under my roof, I command you to make Jesus Christ your Lord and personal savior. If you don't, pack your belongings and leave my house." When I heard what had taken place, I traveled to my father's home to teach the foundational truths of the gospel. I encouraged them not to receive Jesus by force but to believe from their hearts. The entire house and even the neighbors, a total of fifteen people, gave their lives to Christ and were baptized. My older and younger sisters moved to my house to learn about Jesus and joined my church.

Ruhengeri

I've said this before, but to understand this next story, it's important to understand that after the genocide, it was like a devil ravaged my country. There was nothing left, only grieving, brokenness, anger, hatred, and fear. When you saw someone, your mind would automatically think maybe this person will take my life. There was no peace. We did what we could to bring the country together. The government helped, of course, but ministers also helped by interceding. I started fasting. In the beginning, I sought God with a twenty-day fast. I felt so much pain because everywhere I looked, people were in pain. We asked forgiveness for those who killed others. God asked me to talk to other ministers and to form a group because restoring this country would take a team.

I found a few ministers, and we agreed to fast and seek God. We went to the countryside to visit an Anglican church. It was in a part of town considered the "danger zone." People were still being killed due to insurgents. I was the youngest of the group and the only girl. All the other ministers were grown and married men. We were all nervous about visiting such a dangerous place. The atmosphere in the car was tense. It was a three-hour drive. It was common for any visitors traveling that route to be attacked, their vehicles bombed, etc. Right before we approached the most dangerous section, we stopped to dedicate ourselves and the city we were about to enter to God.

As everyone sought God alone, I remember facing a big mountain and crying out, "God! In the name of Jesus, we come before you. We are tired of this killing! They kill people for no reason!"

As I'm praying, I see a spirit in the form of a giant rising from the mountain. He is so big and overwhelming that it is like he is rising out of the mountain itself. He has two big staves in his hands and lifts them up. The whole area seems to quake.

It said to me, "How dare you? Who are you? Why are you here? Do you know my name? I'm the king of this city of Ruhengeri. I drink blood. I sleep on a bed of blood, and I cover myself in blood. I will never stop killing!"

He started coming towards me. He took a step, and it felt like the whole mountain shook. I gasped, opened my eyes, and realized it was a vision. I ran back to the team and told them what I just saw. We piled in the car and did a short prayer, thanking God for revealing to us the principalities holding the whole city. In Ephesians 6:12 (NIV) it says,

> *For our struggle is not against flesh and blood, but against the rulers, against the authorities, against the powers of this dark world and against the spiritual forces of evil in the heavenly realms.*

We thanked God for the victory we had not yet seen. We had faith, and we went forward. I heard the Lord tell me, *"Don't eat any food. Fast until you leave that city."* When we got to the church where we were to hold our service, only two people were there. Only four people attended the next service. In the following service, we had ten people. On Friday, we went to the mayor to ask if we could connect to the loud speakers when driving around the city to let people know we were there and available to pray for them. The mayor was nice. He agreed and even offered the use of the stadium for our service. As we walked out, I felt the Spirit tell me that I shouldn't leave the mayor without sharing the gospel, so I turned and suggested that to the other people on my team.

At this point, the team saw me as an intercessor and as a singer, but not a preacher because I was a woman. Back then, a woman was not allowed to preach, especially not in front of a man. The group didn't want to cause trouble, but the Holy Spirit wouldn't let me leave. I turned to the mayor, grabbed his hands, looked into his eyes, and said, "Today is the day of your salvation! We brought Jesus into your office. Believe in Him like He has believed in you to take care of His people. If you do, you will stay longer in this office. If you don't accept Jesus, you will get kicked out of your place as mayor." He took his glasses off and put them on the table. He kneeled down. I laid my hands on him, and when the other ministers saw him on his knees and me laying hands on him, they hurried back to join me as I led him to Christ.

We used the stadium the following Sunday morning and our last day in the city. We expected just a few people as usual. Initially, just a few people showed up, but all of a sudden, we saw a big group of people coming. We thought the people were coming to kill us. We were so scared that we started asking God to have mercy and to forgive us of any last sins! We thought this was undoubtedly our last day. But as the group got closer, we realized they weren't there to kill us at all! The soldiers went to all of the villages, gathered people from every village in the city, and escorted them to the stadium. The stadium filled up completely! At least 10,000 people came. Everyone came to hear about Jesus! Many people were led to Christ, repented of their sins, and delivered from evil spirits. From that day to today, the city, once known as a "danger zone," is now recognized as a safe place. The mayor is still in office. The Lord answers prayers! Isn't that awesome?

After Ruhengeri, this team started working together to bring reconciliation across Rwanda. God would tell us where idols dedicated to the country were located. God told us to march in the locations of the idols and proclaim freedom and healing for the nation. We declared that no more idols would be dedicated to this country. We proclaimed that no more blood would be shed.

I remember one statue was a hybrid of a human and a bird. This statue was not an expression of art or an innocent gift from another country; it was an idol. We marched in prayer, advocating for the statue to be taken down. Two months after the march, the new, post-genocide government supported the removal of statues as a way to make a fresh start. After that, the government started creating local "reconciliation" leaders, who helped the country come out of darkness. Today, when you come to Rwanda, you can't even tell if a genocide took place. Prayers, with the government's support, helped the country. There was no other way to heal.

The Snake on Stage

Before one of the crusades started, a group of Muslim leaders showed up at the venue in their traditional garments. They cut open a live chicken and poured the blood all over the area where I was supposed to preach. They spoke curses over me and the crusade. They wanted me to step in the chicken blood to die. They didn't know that I follow Jesus, who conquers death! Then, a huge snake slithered to the front a couple hours before the crusade! Everyone screamed. It circled the area I was supposed to preach and menacingly hissed at anyone who was near. Between the blood and the snake, the people knew the Muslims had cursed the area, and they were scared for their lives. They told me to cancel the crusade, but I said, "No. That's just the devil. In the name of Jesus, I'll go." I started walking around the area where the Muslims had been, taking authority in the name of Jesus. I told the worshippers there to begin praising God. By the time the crusade started, the snake was nowhere to be found. No one had killed it. No one had seen it leave; it just vanished.

I preached that night, and the power of God was so strong. People forgot all about the snake. Many people were healed and delivered. Forty-five people gave their lives to Christ. When I called up the Muslim witch doctor woman to testify about how Jesus saved her, eight Muslim leaders dressed in their full garb approached the area with knives to kill us. They didn't want anyone who was a Muslim to become a Christian. They were so angry that this woman who knew all of their secrets was testifying about Jesus. The local security and military had to step in and seize them. The police kept guard over us until the service was over.

When you are attacked, and Jesus is not in your heart, you will be distracted and susceptible to fear, believing the wrong things. When you live with Jesus, the fear will disappear. You will have confidence in Jesus and not fear any spiritual attack. There is NOTHING greater than the blood of Jesus. One sacrifice was made. The Lamb of God takes away all of the curses, all of the sins, and all of the pain of our broken hearts. Nothing is stronger than the name of Jesus when you pray and believe.

Newlywed Bedroom Trouble

One of the men in the town had his eyes on one of the girls from our church. He told the girl he wanted to marry her. We initially objected because he was Muslim, but she felt like he was the one, so we prayed because she insisted. When she made up her mind, we didn't stop her. They married, and their marriage looked like it was going well. After two months, something started to happen. The man could no longer have an erection. The wife was worried. She went back and told us all about it! She said, "If this can't work, then why am I there? He's not functioning! What can I do?" She asked us to talk to God on behalf of her marriage. This same girl had come to me years before asking me to pray for her to have a period. She was turning 30 and had never had a period.

I prayed and told her, "God has delivered you from this pain that you've had for all this time. Just go buy pads and then go home."

She said, "Yeah, I wish, but before she got home, she went to the restroom and realized she was having her period. She forgot we prayed, and she got scared that something was wrong! But it turned out to be the normal period!

Now, she's married, and the husband cannot function. It was so funny and awkward to be praying for a man's erection. I didn't know what words to use, but I tried, and we prayed together. She went back home and called us excitedly, "Friends! It's halfway there! Pray more!" We started praying more, and he became fully erect! She called later and said he made it!! Everything seemed great. However, two days later, her desire diminished. Every time he made an advance, she had no desire for him. Her libido was gone. So she returned to us and said, "Friends, whatever this was, it is now on me! I have no desire for my husband! We have to pray again!" We prayed and her body returned to 100%. Soon after, they had two kids.

Jesus can heal every aspect of our lives! Whenever we think, "Oh, we cannot take it to Jesus," we can! He is with us for everything we walk through and every detail!

Man Healed of HIV

I was preaching on the radio, and God revealed to me that someone was listening who was about to commit suicide. This person felt like he made a mistake so big that he had no choice but to die. Knowing God gave me the revelation for a reason, I started describing what the Lord showed me on the radio. I said there was a man with pills in front of him ready to take his own life. I spoke to him over the radio, "Don't take the pills! Put them down. Meet me now at our church, Rwanda Victory Mission. I'll head there straight from the studio. Come meet me." By the time I showed up, I found a man kneeling at the compound, hands up to God, tears streaming down his face. When he saw me, he said, "Are you Pastor Josephine? I was about to take my life when I heard you speak to me on the radio!" He was still on his knees, his hands trembling as he spoke. "I've been to ten different doctors from different clinics. They've all told me I have HIV. I'm young. I don't want to die that way. Will you pray for me?" I told him his HIV would be like having a headache. A headache goes away after a while, and so would his HIV.

The first prayer was to lead him to Christ, which set the foundation for his faith. Disease is often followed by fear. The devil looks for areas to provoke us and harm our bodies. When fear grabs you, it can consume you to the point where you can't imagine life anymore. That's how the attack happens.

For that reason, I knew this man was struggling with fear. I needed to help him become strong. Romans 8:15 says,

> *For you did not receive the spirit of slavery to fall back into fear, but you have received the Spirit of adoption as sons, by whom we cry, "Abba! Father!"*

We met consistently for prayer and Bible study. I taught him how to seek God, how to fast, and how to pray. I taught him how to cast out devils, cast out sickness in his body, and free his mind from confusion. After three months, I sent him to the doctor for an HIV test. When the results came back, there was NO TRACE of HIV. He couldn't believe it. He wanted to wait another three months and go back again to make sure. Initially, he had gone to ten different doctors who all gave him reports of HIV. Another three months passed, and he went back to the doctor for another test. Again, there was NO TRACE of HIV. He went back multiple times to make sure. The doctors were in disbelief. They had given him the original report of being positive, and now the HIV was gone. He was so thrilled! He told everyone, "Jesus! Jesus healed me!" After some time, he fell in love and proposed to a wonderful woman. They asked me to wed them. He now has a beautiful family and a good job. He is still HIV-free.

The Husband and Pregnant Wife Healed of HIV

There was a young couple who discovered the woman had HIV shortly after moving in together. The husband loved her, and he hated to see his wife suffering. He came to me for prayer. The husband told me not to tell anybody. They were concerned people around them would panic. I would go over to their house often and pray for God to take away the disease and bring total healing. Sometimes, the husband would come and sleep at the church, interceding overnight for her. During this time, she found out she was pregnant. They also were informed the husband had HIV. He got very sick.

While I was on an overseas trip, God said, "*Call him because the spirit of death has come to take him. Speak life over him.*"

At the time, I didn't know he was at the hospital in dire condition. I called a pastor and told them to go to the hospital and put the phone to his ear.

I prayed for him over the phone and said, "I send you home in peace. You are not sick. It's just an attack from the devil, and your body is shutting down. God says I am to speak life to you."

After two days, his body had improved, and they sent him home! He got tested again, and the results came back negative for HIV! The wife decided to finish high school and graduate college. Today, she lives HIV-free. She works for a bank. They have two girls and one boy. None of them have HIV. The mother has tested many times, and the results have kept coming back negative. She started telling others about it six years after continuing to get negative tests.

I've seen eight people healed of HIV. Some people say that miracles are only for the days of Jesus. I'm here to tell you that even today, Jesus is performing miracles when you believe. Sometimes we may have a problem and think it is too big for God, but nothing is bigger than God.

Poisoned by a Hutu Doctor

In 2001, I led seven Muslims to Christ. The Muslim leaders, angered that they were losing people, decided to retaliate. These leaders wanted to hinder me from ministering God's truth to more of their people. They inflicted a sickness on me to kill me. For four months, I was viciously sick. The first thing to go was my voice. My vocal cords were suddenly tired and weak. A whisper took too much effort. I had to stay silent. Then, pain hit my eyes. I couldn't open up my eyelids without experiencing immense pain. I had to keep them closed. My arms and legs became too heavy to move. The sickness set in, and I couldn't talk, see, or move. Yet, despite the paralysis of my physical body, my spirit was strong. I was constantly praying and interceding. I felt like a whole different person.

Even in my condition, people would come to my house and ask me to pray for them, but because I couldn't talk or move, they would take my hand and move it to where they felt their pain. They would say, "I believe you hear me, Pastor. Just pray silently, and I believe God will hear you", and it worked! The Lord healed many people during that time. This amazed me! How could I be so sick and so many people can be healed through my prayer?

I visited two hospitals. They ran exams, and both came back with the same report. My appendix needed to be removed as soon as possible. My intestines were punctured. My liver had a hole. A hole! My kidneys were shutting down. My heart was swollen. This caused great alarm, and the doctors insisted on at least removing the appendix. They said it was about to rupture. At the time, I did not know that this was a spiritual attack on my body, but I did feel, in my spirit, that going into an operation was a trick from the devil, so I refused. Not being able to talk, I would write on a piece of paper to my friends to communicate that I was not willing to go into an operation and take me home.

The night after visiting the second hospital, I had a dream. I watched four men come into my house with a coffin. They opened the coffin. They grabbed a body and started wrapping the body with the white burial linens, but they didn't cover the feet. They were holding the body to place it in the coffin, starting with the head first. Then, I saw the feet and realized that they were MY FEET! I said to the four men, "Hey! How dare you! Where are you taking me? In the name of Jesus, those are my feet. You can't take me away!" I rushed over to fight them, and as I approached, they left my body and ran away. I woke up.

The following morning, my condition had worsened. My friends decided that they had to get me some treatment, so they called a taxi to take me to the clinic. The doctor at the clinic was a Hutu. Now, as you may know, during the Rwandan Genocide, the Hutus sought to exterminate the Tutsis. When the Hutu doctor saw me, he realized I was Tutsi and quickly accepted me into his office. He told everyone else—all my family and friends—that they needed to go out into the waiting room so that it was just him and I together.

As soon as we were alone, he said, "Hey, look at me. I want you to die with this memory." Seeing I couldn't open my eyes on my own, he stretched my eyelids apart with his fingers so I could see him. He said, "Listen to me. We, the Hutus, have not stopped working. When you die, go with this message. Tell your cockroach friends who have died ahead of you that we are still working. We will soon bring even your president down." He mixed a poison in front of me. He said, "Look, this is your goodbye medicine."

I wanted to run away or scream for help, but my voice was gone and my body was too weak. All I could do was pray. I dedicated that poison to God and started claiming Mark 16:18, which says,

...and if they drink any deadly poison, it will not hurt them;

I prayed that the poison would be like dripping water and like a vitamin to my body. I prayed until the poison went to my head, and I passed out. The doctor called my friends to take me and told them the medicine would knock me out for a few hours, but not to worry. He instructed them to take me home, put me to bed, and let me sleep. He wanted to make sure the poison would have time to sink in and kill me altogether. My friends, thinking that I would recover, did just that.

Around 4 am, I had another dream. In the dream, I was standing behind a gathering of people at a graveyard. They were there to say goodbye to someone who had just passed. The priest was dressed formally, saying a few words and reading the scriptures to the people. Then, he said the name of the deceased. When I heard it, I was confused. He said my name, but obviously, I was alive! He then invited the people to come up and say goodbye before putting the body in the ground. I hurried to see the person in the open coffin. As I looked down, I saw my face, lifeless, staring back at me. I SCREAMED, "I can't die! I can't die young! It's not my time to die! I refuse this death!" I started kicking the coffin. I kicked so hard that it fell to the ground and started rolling. I kept kicking it until the coffin opened up completely and my body came out of the coffin. I woke up. I was covered in so much sweat. It was like I had just gotten out of a pool.

From there, I asked God, "This is the second time I saw the coffin. What is going on? Why am I being hunted by the coffins?"

Very clearly, I heard the voice of God say to me, *"Much like the time in the Old Testament when the angel of death was passing by the homes in Egypt and the Israelites had to put the blood of Jesus on their door to protect them, there is a spirit of death going around. Tell the people of your church to fast for four days to receive protection for both them and their families. Their fasting and intercession will stop this spirit of death."*

The following day, I brought the church together and relayed the message. I was still in terrible condition. The church members had to carry me into the church on a bed with pillows to prop me up. I could barely speak but did my best to get the word out. The church started fasting. The first and second days passed. On the third day, something amazing happened. I woke up feeling strong. For the first time in over four months, I could open my eyes without pain. I could hear my own voice. I felt strong! I went to the church and started praying for everyone else I knew!

On the fourth day of the fast, I started preaching, ministering, and laying hands on people. Right then, Jesus said to me, "I want you to go to Belgium." I went to the Embassy, where they gave me the visa, and I bought a ticket. The family I went to visit had two sisters who were both nurses. I showed them the report from my earlier hospital visits. They took me to the doctor and did a full scan. The liver, the heart, the intestines, my kidneys, and even the appendix were all in perfect condition. Every organ in my body was fine. There was only one abnormality. Blood tests picked up large amounts of poison in my body. The nurses put me on a treatment to remove the poison. Within one month, my body recovered completely, and I returned to Rwanda. Upon my return, it was like the fog of death had lifted.

Meeting the Hutu Doctor

Shortly after, I hosted our annual conference. The conference theme was "Faith in Action." My face was on flyers all over the town promoting the event. The Hutu clinic doctor saw my face on the flyers and was in disbelief. He knew I should be dead. He had to see it for himself, so he came to the conference. He didn't want to enter the conference; he stood at a distance! I recognized him and walked up to him. He had his hands on his head, his face struck with shock. I said, "You're the doctor! Do you remember me? It's not my time to die, and I have a message for you—Believe in Jesus as your personal Savior now, and confess your sins for killing many innocent people, and you will be cleared. If you deny Jesus, judgment is waiting for you for the innocent people you've killed." I thought about calling the police on him, but I decided this battle was God's. God will fight for me.

Sometimes, people die before their time. The devil came to kill and to destroy. You may feel sick, and you may feel like, "This is it! I better tell everybody about my disease and sickness, and I will die." Giving into those thoughts will cause the sickness to grow! The medicine for stopping the sickness is having faith in God. That happened in 2001. By this time, it was 2022, and I am alive! None of my organs were affected. I still have my appendix! Whose report shall we believe? We shall believe the report of the Lord!

The Woman With the Issue of Blood

Another woman was having an issue with bleeding. This lady was bleeding so severely and bled for three weeks nonstop. She and her husband were together for several years. They had no children, and the bleeding and pain persisted. Her husband told her to go and remove her uterus to avoid cancer risk. She didn't want to because she still wanted to have a baby.

I don't usually wake up early before church. However, on this morning, I woke up and was at the church by 6 am. I spent the time interceding, and then at 7 am, I started cleaning the compound. We live close to the street where the bus drives by. The woman with the issue of bleeding was on the bus in tears on the way to the doctor. She saw me as the bus drove by. We knew each other, but not well, and she had never told me before about her suffering. She told the bus to stop. She got off to see me because she was worried that the surgery would kill her, and she wanted to say goodbye to someone she knew and receive prayer in case the surgery did not go well. She told me her husband wanted her to do it, but she wanted babies. When she told me, I felt a very deep anger in my spirit.

I exclaimed, "OK, woman! This is not a joke at all. You should not believe the reports of your doctor, and you should not take the orders of your husband because you don't have cancer and you will have babies." I felt the Spirit of God in me and continued, "Listen to me! Which report will you believe? If you take the doctor's report and the husband's order, you will not have babies. Do not go to the doctor. You stay here all day, and I will pray for you. Stay until the evening. When you go home, tell your husband you are healed."

She stayed all day. I prayed for her and prophesied over her, and then I prayed for her and prophesied over her even more. At 5:30 pm, I sent her home. By the time she got home, she noticed the bleeding had stopped. The following day, the bleeding was gone. That same month, she conceived. Nine months later, she had a healthy baby boy. To this day, she calls him "Josephine's son." I have many kids.

Believing in Jesus gives you courage to do things you've never done before. The devil came to kill, steal, and destroy. Being connected to Jesus gives you the power to conquer demons and lead people to Christ, free people living in darkness, and heal and deliver people from viruses and diseases.

Prayer

When a person is a Christian, it's not just about reading the Bible and going to church. It's about much more than that. It's about building a relationship with God. If you learn how to pray, you'll be powerful in the kingdom and learn God's language. You cannot find God any other way but by talking to him through prayer.

In 1 Samuel 2, Hannah shows a determination to seek God. She prays for a child and for the shame of barrenness to be taken away. Her husband's other wife curses her every day, and she has to endure it every morning and every night. But when God hears her prayers, he silences all those who mock her.

1 Kings 18:18-27 talks about Elijah. Elijah was a prayer warrior. The prophets of Baal offered sacrifices for their gods to respond. Elijah prayed. Elijah called the fire, and the fire came down. Fire fell from heaven in response to Elijah's prayers.

In Matthew 7:7, Jesus said,

Ask, and it will be given to you; seek, and you will find; knock, and it will be opened to you.

To me, that means when we speak to God in prayer, our words are knocking on heaven's door. They go straight to God. For those who are wondering how God speaks, it's through prayer. To hear from God, you must be intentional when seeking Him. How can He speak to you when you don't give Him any attention? The world will never leave you alone. You have to carve out time away from people's and life's demands to pray.

Ezekiel 33 talks about watchmen. Our job is to be a watchman. It's about having concern for others. When you pray, you don't pray for only yourself and forget everyone else. Expand your prayers to your neighbors, your church, your enemies, and even those in the hospital! You intercede as a watchman because you want others to be free.

Esther, as found in the book of Esther, demonstrated a good example of what it means to be a watchman when she was told her family was in great danger. She fasted, prayed, and used her position to save her people. Prayer is like a battle. When you pray, you're not fighting in the flesh, you're fighting in the spiritual realm. Take all the weapons, as listed in Ephesians 6:14-17. Prayer is greater than a bomb. Matthew 18:18-19 talks about binding and loosing. You can't bind without being in the battle. You start fighting the battle, and then you bind.

You bind the devil and any unclean spirits. It means you're removing and clearing the way. What you loose is the anointing of God to cover and protect. I identify an evil thing. I bind it. I tell it to get out in the name of Jesus, and then I receive the blood of Jesus and spiritual weapons. There are two types of prayer—one of asking and one is giving thanks for what you've received in Jesus Name.

Don't be discouraged if it doesn't happen immediately. It's less about which words you use and more about having a heart for it. When you pray, don't pray empty words. Pray using the word of God. Scripture is how you connect to heaven. Prayer is not something you do. It must be a part of you, in your bones and blood. Many people may think there are some kinds of prayers God will answer and some kinds of prayers God will not. But God always answers our prayers.

The Man in the Coma for Six Months

I have seen three people resurrected from the dead and eight people who have come back from a coma through the name of Jesus. One of the people in a coma was in a motorcycle accident. When he fell off the bike, the back of his skull slammed against the ground. He was in a coma in the hospital for six months. I had just returned from being gone for a year and was back preaching at my church.

While preaching, God told me that there was someone in the church who had a family member whose condition was so bad that their health was teetering between life and death. I mentioned it to the church and asked the person to please come forward. The son of the man who was in the motorcycle accident was a church member. He came forward and asked me to pray for his father. We went to King Faisal Hospital in Kigali, Rwanda. When we arrived, the father was not responsive. There were a few family members present, and they seemed to be waiting for him to pass away. Everyone was discouraged and broken-hearted. But when I looked at him, I felt the courage to run and pray for him. As I prayed for him, I felt in my spirit that I should call his name and talk to him.

When I called his name, I told him, "I know you're there. Remember, there are people around here who love you and who want to talk to you. I am one of them."

I carried on talking. I commanded him in the name of Jesus to talk to me. I kept praying for his eyes to open and look at me. He looked like he was already gone, but there was a strong faith in me that it was not his time to die.

I squeezed his hand tightly and said, "I want you to look at me. In the name of Jesus, I have great news to share with you."

Fifteen minutes went by, no difference. Around twenty minutes, I noticed movement in his eyelids. I spoke to him and told him that this was not his time to die, and that this was not his time to go to heaven. Then, it started. His hand moved. Then his toes began to wiggle. He started moving his legs in a small kicking motion. Finally, his eyes opened! As he regained consciousness, I continued speaking scriptures over him, like Psalm 91:15-16 (NIV):

He will call on me, and I will answer him; I will be with him in trouble, I will deliver him and honor him. With long life I will satisfy him and show him my salvation."

I requested for someone to bring over something for him to drink. He began to drink and looked around the room and recognized his son and daughter in the room with him. They asked him if he knew who they were. He said, "Of course!" and greeted them by name. From there, he started talking. He was in high spirits. He acted like he had just arrived at a party! I have never seen anyone wake up so quickly and completely! One by one, his family members hugged him and began to cry. After four days, he was released from the hospital.

Another Coma Story

An older gentleman, over sixty at least, got sick and asked his daughter, Olivia, to take him to the hospital. The medicine the doctors prescribed made his condition worse. He became weaker and weaker until he eventually ended up in a coma. The hospital sent him home to die. Olivia asked me to pray for him. I felt that I should bring the choir from our church and worship. We worshiped in the living room, and after a while, I felt we should enter his bedroom. We began worshiping and praying in tongues. I felt in my spirit that I should lay my hands on his ears and eyes, and I started calling his name.

I told him, "We're here to fellowship with you. I know you're there. You can hear us. You can't talk, but you can hear us."

I commanded him three times in the name of Jesus to talk. His thumb began moving. I continued praying in tongues for a few more minutes, and he began opening his eyes and started yawning. The family had previously said that, in his state, he could not eat or drink. I requested that someone bring him something to drink. Someone brought him orange soda. He started sipping slowly. He then started making sounds, which turned into words! He began sharing how happy he was to wake up to the sound of worship. His daughter and the rest of his family were thrilled to see their father awake.

I have seen more, but there is not enough space in the book to tell you all the stories about people Jesus brought out of a coma after our prayers. I am here to encourage you. When you are about to lose your faith, don't be mad at God. Don't be angry. Just ask because everything you ask in the name of Jesus shall be given unto you. In John 14:13-14 (NIV) Jesus says,

> *And I will do whatever you ask in my name so that the Father may be glorified in the Son. You may ask me for anything in my name, and I will do it.*

The Man Who Thanked Me After Death

I was invited to pray for a man at his house. This man was very wealthy and had a big family with lots of sons and daughters. When I walked in, my heart broke. The man's body was completely paralyzed. I looked at him and said, "Sir, it looks like you have come to your end, but don't lose hope. Jesus can heal you." That day, I told him about Jesus. I visited his house daily to bring him medicine through the Word of God. Then I would lay my hands on him and pray. Every time I laid hands on him, I would see a little improvement. When I met him, he was bedridden and drinking food through a straw. After a few days, he was sipping soup with a spoon. Then, he was able to eat sitting properly. Eventually, he could stand up and walk while leaning on the walls. Finally, he started walking by himself. The man, who had completely lost control of his body, was now walking on his own! He started saying, "If Jesus can do this, other people must need help like me. I want to help them. I don't know how to preach, but I have vehicles, drivers, and resources."

He offered to finance our evangelism work. Everything he supported, he wanted to be a part of. He wanted to be there with us. His car would pull up to pick us up for evangelism, and he'd be the first to get in. There would sometimes be three vehicles to fit him, his family, and the teams. He would provide the gas, the food, and anything else as long as he could be a part of it. This went on for several months. He would tell me, "Never ever, ever leave me! You were sent to this earth for me. If you leave me, that's when I'll die." I'd tell him not to say things like that. One time, he decided he wanted to be baptized in water. When his family heard, they were embarrassed that an important and well-known man like him would be willing to be publicly baptized by a woman. They told him his health was too fragile.

He said, "It's my decision. If I die, I die."

When they couldn't convince him, they threatened me instead. I told them I only answered to God. The baptism was made to be a huge celebration!

He came out of the water and exclaimed, "Victory!! I made it!!"

Later on, I was invited to Europe for a couple of weeks to preach. He was devastated.

"Don't go! What if I die?" he begged.

I told him, "Don't worry. I must go. People are waiting."

He cried.

On my third night in Europe while I'm sleeping, I hear someone say in Rwandese, excitedly, "My Pastor! Thank you so much for showing me Jesus! You can't believe how great it is to be with Jesus! I'm with Him now! Thank you!" I recognized that voice. In the morning, I called my people in Rwanda. They told me that the man had passed the same night I had the dream. They told me he died while looking up to heaven smiling and telling everyone, "Look! Do you see what I see? Do you see them worshiping?" Of course, no one else could hear.

It's good to walk with the Lord. Even when you come to the door of death, you won't be afraid because you'll know where you're going. Death is a transformation from this life to another life. If you've prepared your way with Jesus, you take comfort knowing your name is registered in the "Book of Life." The angels will accompany you to his throne. They will be right there to take you straight to your King. I beg you to walk with God till your last day.

The Infertile Cows

There was a woman who was married for four years with no kids. In African culture, you don't marry a woman without giving honor to the parents. For example, the groom will give the parents a tangible gift, like a cow. In this case, the groom gave the parents two cows for the wedding. During the first four years, even those two cows could not reproduce. She came to me and said, "I beg you! Woman of God, if anyone is in trouble, it's me. I cannot have a child, and even the cows given to my parents cannot reproduce!" I prayed for her and told her there was a curse on her. We needed to lay hands on her and the cows and in doing so, the curse would be broken. She told her family, and they invited me to their home to pray. I laid hands on the cows and laid hands on the woman. Within a few months, the woman conceived and the cows did too! They even gave birth around the same time! This woman now has three children. This is an example of what God can do when you pray.

When I Was Face to Face With a Leopard

I set aside three days of fasting day and night. During this time, I would separate myself from distractions and sit somewhere I could be alone to focus on prayer and reading my Bible. I found a secluded, wooded area. On the third day, during the day time, I heard behind me the sound of sticks snapping. I turned around, and a leopard was baring its teeth at me and hissing, poised to jump on my neck. The teeth were hideous. I can see them even today. I closed my eyes so I wouldn't see myself die and screamed JESUS!!! I screamed it as loud as I could! I screamed again. JESUS!!! I kept my eyes closed, waiting to be eaten. I didn't move; I didn't open my eyes. I was sitting there frozen, waiting for something to happen but nothing happened! When I opened my eyes, I was no longer in the garden. I was staring at the front door of the church. The church was about a quarter of a mile from where I saw the leopard. And yet, somehow, without walking or getting up or anyone carrying me, I was not in the wooded area anymore but in front of the church! I was in shock! How did I end up here? What happened to me? This is unbelievable! How will I explain this? Then I remembered the story in the Bible about Philip and the Ethiopian man.

Philip was transported to the Ethiopian man who was in the chariot reading the scriptures, and, consequently, Philip led him to Christ (Acts 8:29-39). God has many ways of rescuing his people. God rescued me from being killed by that horrible leopard. When I called on the name of the Lord, I was transported straight to the church door and found safety. There was nothing special about my prayer; I just called on Jesus.

Jeremiah 33:3 says,

Call to me and I will answer you.

I called on Jesus, and He answered my prayer.

The Mother Controlled by Her Sister

I was preaching at the Full Gospel Businessmen's Conference. A mother who had received Christ invited me to her house after the service. I started praying a blessing and greeting the house with the prayers. She brought her two teenage children, a girl and a boy, to greet me. I reached out and touched the daughter on the shoulder. When my hand touched her shoulder, God showed me what took place in the daughter's life.

I looked at the mother and said, "I have something to tell you."

The mother sent her kids away so we could be alone. I said, "One of your relatives has claimed your daughter to be her own. Even if you have her here physically in your house, she's not fully yours. That relative lives really close by, not far from you at all."

The mother looks at me and says, "Yes! My neighbor is my sister and she's the one who has claimed my daughter."

We started praying. The mother responded to the prayer in an unusual way. Her voice changed completely to a different voice. She started throwing up uncontrollably. The power of God was so strong it caused the evil spirits in her to manifest. Then, there was an unexpected hard knock on the door.

The person knocking was yelling, "Open the door! Open the door! Open the door!"

The mother, who was still vomiting, started crawling on the floor until she could turn the door handle. The sister was at the door!

She told the mother, "We cannot let her take authority here. We cannot accept Jesus in this house. Look at me! Don't you know your daughter is mine? This is not a surprise to you. Come with me."

It was like the mother was transfixed. She nodded her head in compliance with everything her sister said. I told them again to believe in Jesus, but the sister said, "Oh, I don't think so. We need to go." The sister pulled the mother out of the house and into the car. But they were so paralyzed by the power of God that they couldn't even drive away. They just sat there. I had nothing else to do but take my purse and leave.

You cannot bring Jesus into someone's life against their will. Jesus came as the light. In John 1:4-5 (NIV, emphasis added), it says,

In him [Jesus] *was life, and that life was the light of all humankind. The light shines in the darkness, and the darkness has not overcome it.*

Sometimes you enter into a battle, but the people you're fighting for aren't willing to accept Jesus. We used to go to cities to hold crusades, and the cities would kick us out and say they didn't need us. Even in the time of Jesus and the disciples, there were places where they were rejected and persecuted. If you ever share Jesus and you don't understand why people resist it, it's not your part to force them. Your only job is to share Jesus with them. You bless them with the blessings of God, and you carry on. Don't be offended, and don't stop doing what you know is right. You leave it in the hands of God and trust God will bring them close at the right time.

People in Chains

After the Genocide, people were traumatized by what happened. They couldn't take it anymore, and it affected them mentally. I remember one guy around nineteen years old who was brought to me in chains and naked. If you tried to put clothes on him, he would tear them off. The people asked me, "Can you help us? He's been in chains for three days." I prayed for him, and a calm came over him. He looked up at me, and started yawning and stretching like he was waking up from a nap. He was clear-headed. When I asked him what was going on, he said he would have hallucinations of the people who killed his family, and that they were after him, too. He said when he would have these hallucinations, it felt like the clothes were getting in the way. He's now free from that torment. He's married, has a family, and has not had an episode since.

In Mark chapter 5, there is a man who was tormented by spirits. He was naked and in chains, and no one could hold him. Jesus commanded the spirits to leave, and after that, the guy was free. When people ran to see what was going on, the guy was clothed and calmly sitting at the feet of Jesus.

The Woman at the Wedding

I was at the wedding of a church member's daughter, and many people were invited. As we were waiting for the ceremony to begin, one of the women in the crowd stood up and screamed. As she screamed, her eyes rolled back and the color of her skin turned pale. She defecated herself. She collapsed on the floor. Everyone just looked, stunned. I didn't even wait to see what happened. As soon as I heard the noise, I jumped from where I was sitting and stood over her. I yelled for everyone to get out of the way. Everyone was looking at me, but I didn't notice. My focus was on the woman. I propped up this unconscious woman with her head and shoulders against my legs and started speaking loudly in tongues. With authority, I commanded the spirit of death to come out.

I said, "You cannot take her! It's not her time. You cannot take her in the name of Jesus! Devil, you must leave." I started commanding in the name of Jesus for her to come back to life. I told her, "Receive your freedom; you are free! Sit up!"

Suddenly, her eyes fluttered open. She looked at me and looked at herself and saw she had defecated herself and been a spectacle in front of everyone at this wedding. She was mortified. When everyone saw that she was awake and fine, everyone came closer to look. The women at the wedding helped to get her to a place where she could change her clothes.

This reminds me of a story in 2 Kings 4:11-36. The son of a family who once hosted Elisha died. The woman did not stop to tell her husband. She didn't even cry. Instead, she went straight to Elisha. When she got near him, she wouldn't leave until he agreed to help. Elisha went back to her house, locked himself inside, and prayed until God brought the boy back to life. When the things that belong to us are being taken away, we should not just stand by and watch. In Christ, we know we have the authority. We must stand up and fight.

Chapter 12

Miracles in Europe

The Plane Crash

God told me I would be going to Europe, but I first needed to fast for nine days. The first three days were not easy! I gave in and ended up eating. As I ate, I hear God's voice say, "*How dare you? I told you to stop eating. Now you must start over again*."

That night, I had a dream. I saw myself on the ground looking at the sky. A plane was flying overhead and the plane caught on fire. A suitcase fell from the plane to my feet. To my surprise, it was MY suitcase! God then explained to me that principalities were rising to take my life, and I needed to fast to clear my death. I started fasting again!

I was headed to Denmark from Namibia, and on my departure date, my ride took me to the airport two hours early. When I arrived, I heard my name announced over the intercom. For some reason, my ticket was switched to another flight. The flight I was initially supposed to take crashed into another plane in the air and fell into the Indian ocean. I couldn't believe it. I didn't realize fasting would clear my way. That solidified in my mind that fasting was essential.

The Lady Who Hadn't Stood Up in Thirty Years

A handicapped lady was brought to a meeting in Ukraine where I was the guest speaker. I didn't see her come in. We were worshiping, and they introduced me to preach. When I stood up to minister, I forgot all the English words I knew! Whenever I tried to talk, it was in my hometown language, Rwandais. This wasn't good because I had a translator who could only translate English! I didn't know what to do, so I started praying in tongues and waving my hands to pray. Everyone started praying in tongues with me.

I was asking God, "What is next? What am I going to do?"

Then, I clearly heard, "*I want you to walk to the back of the church.*"

Now, this place is packed. I had to leave my interpreter on the stage. When I started walking, I didn't know where I was heading. I just kept walking, and the people had to get out of the way to let me go. Far in the back, there was a woman who was sleeping on a cot. When I got close to her, I felt like I should stop and talk to her. I could tell she was sick, but I didn't know what was going on with her.

The English words started returning to my mind, "What are you doing? Everyone is worshiping, and you're sleeping."

She responded in her language but I didn't understand what she said.

I just looked back at her and, in English, said, "No, you cannot sleep. Stand up. Give me your hand."

She gave me her hand. She stood up; it seemed instinctive. She acted like she forgot that she had never stood up in her life! For thirty years, she was bedridden and only moved for people to change her sheets. She had never stood on her feet for a single day. Standing up, I told her to walk with me to the stage and preach with me. When she got to the stage, it hit her all at once. She was healed! She could now, for the first time, stand and walk! The whole church went crazy and the woman was so excited!

In her whole life, all thirty years, she had never stood alone and now she was standing, walking, and jumping. That is God. Through prayer, God can give you back your legs! God can give you the desires of your heart! God can fix things you think are too late. He can fix it in a snap. That woman had the victory, and after her miracle, many miracles took place because the people realized that it could happen to them too! There were many, many miracles! There was not even time to receive everyone's testimonies because there were so many because of the presence of God. I encourage you to have faith in God. It will help you when you are in trouble and need him.

Travel Officials Required Papers I Didn't Have

From Ukraine, I took a plane to Germany. When we landed, all the police officers stood at the doors with a mega horn saying, "Ladies and Gentlemen, if you are not a citizen and you do not have a visa, remain sitting. The officers are coming to check on you." I did not have a visa. I was passing through on my way to Denmark. The German people did not want any strangers without a transit visa. The team I went with to Denmark told me I was in trouble because I was a black woman and would stick out to them. They could have sent me back to Ukraine. I told them to stop talking like that because God will take care of me, and I'm not going back. I'm going home. I told them to stand behind me and not to talk to me anymore and told them to let me pray. I got into the line with the people with visas.

My friends told me to sit down, but I said, "No! Watch, my king will take care of me. Who will stop me?"

I went forward in the line while I was praying in tongues. I got close to the officer and handed him my passport while smiling.

As I handed him my passport, in another language, I said, "I blind your eyes in the name of Jesus."

He thought I was saying hello and said hello back! He looked at my passport, handed it back to me, and approved it. And that was it! I went straight down the stairs from the plane, and I started dancing! I waited for my team to come, and as they came down the stairs, they were shaking their heads! They wouldn't talk to me for a long time. I said, "Where is your faith?" Romans 8:31 says,

If God is for us, who can be against us?

The whole world belongs to God.

The Woman Who Was Paralyzed in the Hip For 12 Years

In Denmark, there was a woman who had been paralyzed by cancer. She was in a wheelchair. As I was preaching, it suddenly felt like my hip socket was falling apart. I said to the crowd, "Who's been paralyzed in the hip for twelve years?" They pushed this woman forward to where I was. I commanded the woman, "In the name of Jesus, I don't want you to sit and watch me! I want you to jump out of the wheelchair, run, and do things you've never done before." Immediately, she took off! She jumped out of her chair, ran out of the entrance of the building, and ran back in! She was out of breath. After twelve years in a wheelchair, Jesus pushed her out of the wheelchair. God healed her cancer and bones in an instant.

The Man Who Was Deaf and Mute

I moved to another church in Denmark where I met a couple. Both of them were deaf and mute. They came to me for prayer. They tried to tell me their request via sign language, but I couldn't understand. Someone intervened to tell me what they were saying. Once I understood, I realized they were asking for prayer to be healed.

I turned to the husband first and said, "I command the deaf spirit to come out!"

As soon as I did, the husband responded, "OW!!"

I asked "What? Can you talk to me?"

He said, "It's so loud!"

I continued, "What do you hear?"

He said, "I hear everything!!"

Then the wife sees a change, and she gets so excited! She couldn't believe her husband could hear and was talking! The woman started pulling my hands to get me to pray for her, too! So I prayed for her and she was also healed. It reminded me of when Jesus healed a man who was deaf and mute. In Mark 7:35 (NKJV), Jesus prayed for a man and it says,

> *Immediately his ears were opened, and the impediment of his tongue was loosed, and he spoke plainly.*

The Man With the Kidney Problem

In the same service, there was a guy with a kidney problem. I said, "I command the kidneys now to come back to life!" When I said that, he flew back. I walked up to him and again said, "I command your kidneys to come back to life." When he woke up, he said he no longer felt any pain. After a week, he came to see me where I was staying to testify that he no longer had a kidney problem. Jesus, the one who heals the kidney, can also heal the whole body.

The Woman Without a Uterus

Oral Roberts said "Nothing good comes from the devil. Nothing bad comes from God." As Christians, we live by faith, which is our weapon to overcome the enemy. The enemy came to kill and destroy. That is all he does. I remember this woman in Denmark. I was scheduled to preach. They put the advertisement on TV for my preaching location, and this woman was lying in the hospital and saw the commercial for my crusade meetings. She was inspired because the commercial encouraged people to bring the sick, the blind, and the dead. The woman was filled with faith and decided she needed to go. She was so determined to go but it was the day after her surgery. She came to the crusade by ambulance.

Imagine preaching and seeing the ambulance coming up! They put this woman in a wheelchair and pushed her towards the pulpit. I looked at her and wondered what's going on with this woman, but there was no time to ask because I was in the middle of a message. It ended, and I invited people to come up front for prayer. Immediately, she was pushed to the front near me for prayer. I avoided her and prayed for the other people, but they kept pushing her to be before me.

While avoiding her, I asked God, "God, why did this woman come in the ambulance? What's going on?"

But the Lord didn't tell me. Finally, I turned to her to pray. As I opened my mouth, words I had not expected to speak came out.

I said, "Woman, you have cried, and your tears have reached out to God. Next time I see you, I will see you with your babies."

She didn't say anything; she just cried. What I didn't know when I said this was that the woman had her uterus removed the day before! I just prayed for her, and I left her with the message. I went home.

Three years later, I came back to minister in the same location. When I went to this church, there was a couple with two kids, each parent holding one kid. They stood at the back of the church the whole time, smiling and waving at me. I didn't recognize them and was annoyed that these people wouldn't sit down during the preaching!

They came up to me afterward, and the woman said, "Pastor, do you remember me? You may not remember, but you prayed for me. You said the next time you see me, I would be with babies. Now I am here. I want you to know God answered your prayers. I have two babies from my own womb."

She started telling me the story. She became pregnant. She was shocked and hid it. She went to a different doctor than the one who performed the surgery. After she had the second baby, she visited the doctor who took out her uterus. The doctor did not and could not believe it. He was stunned. She wanted him to see the miracle. She named both babies Josephine! Josephine 1 and Josephine 2! The doctor wanted to see the woman who prayed for her. He asked to see me on my next trip to Denmark. He came and brought three other doctors with him.

They asked me, "How do you create a uterus in a person? What's your special medicine?"

"How many times have you done this?" I responded, "I don't do that."

He said, "Yes, you did! Because this woman had no uterus, and now she has two kids. Can you explain that to me?"

I explained the power of our Lord Jesus's resurrection to him and the three other doctors. I explained that God can fix broken bones, heal the blind and deaf, and do anything in Jesus' name. I ended up leading them all to Christ.

The Church Elder With Bad Knees

In Denmark, a church elder in a wheelchair was brought to the front of the auditorium. She was seated near the stage where I was about to preach. When I took the microphone, I noticed her and experienced a sensation like what Jesus must have felt when he saw merchants selling goods in the temple and overturned their tables. It stirred a deep feeling inside me—enough was enough, and action needed to be taken! Before beginning my sermon, I approached the woman and asked her to rise from her wheelchair.

She said, "I can't. My knees! The cancer keeps me from walking."

I told the woman enough was enough. I helped her up, and we took small steps to the stage and back. I whispered in her ear to keep going, and we walked past the stage to the entry door. Everyone was standing with their mouths open. We did it seven times!

I said, "Look around. Do you need the wheelchair?"

She exclaimed, "Oh my gosh! Can I give you a hug?"

Again I asked, "Do you need the wheelchair?"

She replied, "For what?"

That was the end of that wheelchair! She donated her wheelchair to the church and never used it again!

Suicidal Woman at Amsterdam Airport

I was in the Amsterdam airport one day while traveling. There was a woman desperate for someone to talk to. As people walked by, she would reach out and even grab at some of the jackets of the people passing by. She pleaded with them to talk to her. She kept saying that she was going to die and needed to talk to someone now! I had about four hours before my departure. After watching many people brush her off, she said she was about to kill herself. I listened as she continued telling me her story.

I interrupted, "Sit down. Let me talk to you. I have the answer. You've tried relationships, money, and friends, but none worked. It's all gone. But there is one best friend who is left—one who longs to meet you and loves you. A friend lies with you when you are in bed sick. He loves you and is the only one who is there for you. He can heal the broken heart and the wounds you carry on the inside. He can fix the mess of your heart."

She inquired, "Who??"

I simply replied, "Jesus."

She began to cry. Her heart seemed to contract and expand as she realized the love of God. I prayed for her. She became so soft. I felt so much for her. I wanted to take her with me in my suitcase! But I had to leave her to get on the plane. I hugged her and we said a tearful goodbye.

Three years later, while I was preaching in Brussels, a woman came up to me and asked if I remembered her. I wasn't sure if I did. She reminded me about the Amsterdam airport. She said she was suicidal, and I led her to Christ. She became a minister. I was shocked. This woman, who was so desperate and broken, shined with happiness and was spending her life helping other people. If God can heal her broken heart, my friend, He can do it for you!

The Ambassador With the Injured Leg

When I was in Belgium, one of the staff members invited me to a prayer meeting held at the Embassy of an African country. We met during the lunch hour. It was a big group. When I started ministering, the presence of the Holy Spirit was very strong. People were filled with the Holy Spirit, and others were delivered. When the time was up, the ambassador opened the door and peeked in to find everyone lying on the floor, like in a trance. It sparked her curiosity. She called me to her office so she could get to the bottom of what happened during that meeting. She wanted to know what I had done to her people.

Bodyguards guarded her office. They wouldn't let me in without first getting her permission. She told them she would only give me five minutes. When I walked in, she was seated, and her tone was harsh.

"So, you're the one!" she said. "What was that? Can you explain why everyone was lying on the floor and you were the only one standing?"

I asked if I could pray first before I answered. She agreed. As I prayed, God revealed to me that she had terrible pain in her leg and she needed to be healed. God told me the cause of the pain in her leg.

I looked at her and explained, "May I tell you what God is showing me? On your left leg, you have pain. It has been that way for a long time. The pain started while you were down on the first floor."

I gave a few more details, including how many years it's been. Her eyes got wide.

She shrieked, "WAIT! Who told you? Do you have medicine?"

I said, "I can pray for you."

She said, "If you can take away the pain, I would like you to pray for me. Let me close the door first."

She closed the door to her office, and as she was doing it, I could see that she had a limp.

I laid my hands on her and claimed, "In the name of Jesus, be healed."

She shook and then was very still. I started to rebuke the Devil and his demons by telling them to come out in Jesus' name. I commanded them to let her go and get out. She opened her eyes and relaxed but was sweating. The pain in her leg was completely gone. I was supposed to be there for five minutes, but I was there for forty-five minutes! The bodyguards, by that point, were knocking on the door, getting ready to bust in. She had to tell them everything was okay. She wanted to know where I lived, so she could come back and visit anytime. She took me home in her convoy of vehicles from the Embassy. It was so cool to ride with an ambassador. Imagine what God can do! One minute, you're walking on your own feet to get everywhere, and the next minute, you're in an ambassador's convoy! God is awesome. She was completely and instantly healed that day. Jesus can heal our broken bodies. He has the spare parts in heaven! Anything we ask, it shall be given. God ordered a spare part for her to be able to walk and be completely free.

Friends, I know God can heal all kinds of diseases in our bodies. I believe that when you pray, God has spare parts for every part of your body. In Isaiah 59:1 (NIV), it says,

> *Surely the arm of the Lord is not too short to save, nor his ear too dull to hear.*

Nothing is too hard for God!

The Guy in Denmark Who Spoke Namibian

When I first started going on mission trips to Denmark, people did not believe in demons. They kept asking me, "Pastor, have you ever seen demons? I hear there are lots of demons in Africa!"

I would ask, "What about here?"

They replied, "No, no, no, not here! We don't have them here!"

I said, "Just wait—you'll see." I joked that their demons wear suits, just like them. They had a hard time believing me.

While in Denmark, I was invited into a church. When they introduced me, everyone was sitting down quietly. A guy who had never been to that church before and no one knew stood up. He started cursing me in Namibian, an African language. He was a white guy who looked like your typical Danish guy! I was just coming from Namibia, so I was familiar with the Namibian language but didn't know enough to know the words. The Holy Spirit started interpreting what he was saying to me.

He was pointing at me. "You! You are not welcome here! You cannot change anyone in this country! Go back to where you came from! This is my territory!"

Everyone in the church was terrified. It was obvious something was wrong. However, I started laughing. I told everyone what he was saying, and then I said to him, "In the name of Jesus, I rebuke you, devil!"

When I said that, he started running. He ran out of the church and the ushers ran after him. But no one could find him. They looked for him in the bathrooms; he wasn't there. They checked the parking lot; he was not there. He was gone. After that, everyone was scared and turned their attention to God. The rest of the service was really powerful. People started coming from everywhere to attend these services. There were many healings and many miracles.

My message here is to encourage you to always put on the armor of God and be aware that you're in a battle. Ephesians 6 says our battle is not against flesh and blood. It's spiritual. When you put on the armor of God and recognize spiritual warfare, you can be a help to someone. You can be the answer when people don't know what to do.

The Girl Who Tried to Toss Me Out of a Window

I was invited to Belgium and planned to stay with a church member's sister while I was there. After my flight landed, I arrived at the house around 8 pm. The mother of the house opened the door to greet me. Before I could even say hello, my eyes went straight to a large picture hanging opposite the front door. It was a family portrait. The father in the portrait seemed to come to life. His image emerged from the picture like he was standing in front of me! He was angry. I could feel an evil presence. Quietly, I stared at the picture and started telling the picture that it couldn't harm me. As I was speaking, the daughter, who was in her bedroom, ran out to the family room stark naked! She was big-boned and about 6 feet tall. Completely unaware of her nudity, she commanded in an angry, loud tone, "What's going on here? What is happening here?"

She turned to her mom, grabbed her, and lifted her above her head. When I saw her lift the mom, I pushed the couch forward, and the mom landed on the couch when the daughter tried to slam her to the ground. The girl was even angrier when I saved the mom. She exclaimed "How dare you! I will kill you. I will take your eyes!"

At the time, I had very long braids down my lower back. She grabbed my braids, pulled me down, and wrapped the braids around her thigh. She took her other hand and tried to gouge my eyes out. I kept thrashing my head and used my hands to protect my face. She pulled my braids so hard that the hair on the side of my head and the skin with it came off. Blood started running everywhere. I have the scar to this day. When she pulled that hair, it hurt so badly that I realized I needed to fight back. Just being on the defensive and trying to break free wasn't working. But then I heard God say to me clearly, *"Because of the anointing on your life, if you fight back, she will die. Don't do anything. I have not given you this anointing to kill."*

I didn't want to be in a foreign country dealing with a dead body. I yelled "Police! I'm going to call the Police!"

She said, "Whoa, you're going to call the police?"

She got up and started frantically disconnecting all of the phones and wires in the house so that I could not make a call. I saw that as my moment to get away. I ran down a hallway and locked myself in her mom's bedroom. The daughter was screaming as she was making her way down the hall. The door came crashing down. It was a real evil. When she broke the door down, I thought to myself, where am I going to go? She's going to kill me. I saw a window open to a tiny balcony. I jumped on the bed, opened the window, crawled through the window, and onto the tiny balcony. I didn't realize I was on the sixth floor. She saw what I did and claimed that I would be dead and laying on the street below.

She went to the kitchen, where the door to the balcony is, and met me on the balcony. I look down to the street below. I'm already afraid of heights. She's marching towards me, still naked, ready to grab me and throw me onto the street. I was terrified. I jumped back through the window to get back into the house. I'm halfway in, but then she grabs me by the leg. She slams my shin against the window sill. In all my life,

I have never known such pain. I still have the scar. I managed to pull my leg loose. She could not fit in the window, so she had to go back to the balcony door to get into the apartment. I hobbled out of the bedroom, and out of the apartment into the long corridor to find somewhere to go. It was late. All the lights were turned off and I didn't know where I was going.

"Where are you?" she cried.

She switched on light after light in the corridor until she saw me and caught up to me. She started dragging me back to the apartment. This whole time, I wasn't fighting back. I'm only running for my life. I was tired of not fighting. I thought to myself what the point of an anointing was if you can't use it to help protect yourself. I prayed to God to take away the anointing so that I could fight back against this woman. I told God if I fight back and she dies, it is on Him and not me. I believed God heard my prayer. I shoved her hard. She lost her balance. I balled up my hand into a fist and punched her in the back. She yelled in pain and fell to the floor. Her eyes closed, and she just laid there. She was so still I thought I might have killed her. I panicked, thinking everyone was going to find me with a dead person and kill me. I had nowhere to hide. I didn't even know which apartment was theirs to hide in.

I went to her and commanded her to come back to life in the name of Jesus. Moments later, she woke up. She was not dead, but I wondered what caused her to fall asleep. When she woke, she seemed like an entirely different person. She didn't know who I was, why she was in the hallway, why she was naked, and why I was bleeding. She was bewildered. She stood up, went back into the apartment, and left me be. I walked to the elevator and took it to the bottom floor to try and find the mother. The mother had called the police, and they had just arrived. They followed me back up to the sixth floor, only to find the daughter asleep peacefully in bed. They thought we were crazy for calling.

That night, I had nowhere to go. I had to stay the night there. The mom was mortified at what had happened to me. I realized this family needed Jesus. The daughter didn't come out of her bedroom. When she did, she seemed really ashamed. She left the house and was gone for days. The mother was worried and started to panic. I interceded for her. I told the Lord that if she returned while I was still at the house, I knew she would give her heart to Jesus. The next day she came back. I ministered to her, and she, her brother, and the mother all gave their hearts to Jesus. Though they had decided to follow Jesus, they were still suffering from different issues.

Ministry to the Family

I stayed with this family for about a week and kept praying over them. God then showed me what was keeping them bound. God gave me a vision of a black gate with chains. This gate represents where the father dedicates his two kids and wife to his gods. As I prayed, the black gate's chains broke first, and the whole gate door broke. In the vision, I entered that place to rescue the family. As we were leaving through the broken gate, I saw the father in the vision. He screamed and protested. He explained that he had dedicated them to serve his gods without his family knowing. He wanted to keep it that way. By that point in the vision, it was too late. The gate was already broken.

I told the family what I saw in the vision. That's when they realized that they were under a curse. They wanted to break that curse through Jesus.

Soon, the evidence of God's freedom became apparent. When I met the mother, her legs were swollen with water, and her knees were so big it caused her pain. After prayer, she was healed. The brother was also healed from severe asthma. The daughter was born again and baptized. She got her own apartment and went back to school. She hadn't been able to go to school since she was ten. She was now twenty-four. The mom saw her kids grow up and become their own people. Now, they all go to church. The siblings eventually came to visit me in Rwanda. The brother wedded in Africa. I baptized their mom in Africa. After being baptized, the mother's asthma and allergies left. See what Jesus can do!

Deliverance

Spiritual deliverance can heal someone without me even knowing they're going through deliverance. When I knocked the girl down, she was delivered of many demons. She wasn't delivered from all the spirits at once but was delivered from the spirit that was causing her to want to kill me and kept her from realizing she was naked. When I entered the house, I knew it was covered with evil spirits. This experience reminded me of the demons of King Saul. When evil spirits attacked King Saul, David would worship, and demons would flee. Saul would then be peaceful or calm. Everywhere we go, we should walk with Jesus. We should put Jesus first. If someone is struggling with something strange, and you don't understand what's happening in your house, you should know it is the devil himself. Find someone to pray for you, and in Jesus' name, you will be okay.

If you're a Christian, the devil doesn't have power over you. Your body is no longer a house of the devil—he can't just jump in whenever he wants. The house is now occupied and clean. Yet, your weaknesses open doors for the devil to come in and attack. The devil will find and try to exploit your weakness to gain power over you. It is so hard to close that door. As you know, Jesus cannot force himself to enter into your life until you welcome Him in. Deuteronomy 30:15-16 (NKJV) says,

> *See, I set before you today life and prosperity, death and destruction. For I command you today to love the Lord your God, to walk in obedience to him, and to keep his commands, decrees and laws; then you will live and increase, and the Lord your God will bless you in the land you are entering to possess.*

Chapter 13

Miracles in Uganda

I was in a town in West Uganda planning a weeklong conference. I had been in town for four days telling people about the conference, and I faced a lot of resistance from the people. Two religions were already in the town: the Catholic church and the Anglican church. Everyone claimed to be Catholic or Anglican and wasn't open to anything else. There was no breakthrough. I prayed for people, but no miracles took place.

Discouraged, I retreated to the bush to fast and pray. I wondered if I had heard God wrong about going to this place and wanted to be released to go back. As I bow down in prayer, I feel someone tap on my shoulder. I turned around, and there was this tall giant spirit in the form of a human body. It was so tall its head touched the sky. He was laughing at me and telling me I was in the wrong place and he owned the town. He warned me to leave immediatcly. I was terrified. His head was tiny in the sky, but his body seemed eternal. Only one phrase came to my mouth. "In the name of Jesus, by the blood of Jesus, I am covered, and I command you devil to go far away."

When I said that phrase, the giant spirit seemed to deflate like a balloon releasing air. When it was totally deflated, it went "poof!" and vanished into smoke. I was totally amazed by the power of God. I lifted my hands and said, "Now I know I have the victory! That guy was the principality holding the whole city."

When I returned from the bush where I was praying, I found a crowd of people from town searching for me! They wanted me to preach to them. Someone allowed me to use a building that held 500 people freely, so I had a meeting place. I will never forget that day.

It reminds me of Daniel, who fasted and prayed. He didn't get his answer at first because principalities were in the way, holding his blessings captive. The principalities of darkness can't win. Jesus built the bridge and entrusted us with the keys of authority.

The Man With the Generational Curse

The following day, there was a forty-three-year-old man who was bound in chains because he had a mental illness. He always ran around naked in the street. His whole town knew him. His family decided to go and bring him. The family said there was nothing they could do. Six people were needed to restrain him physically, and they brought him straight to my house! They didn't want to wait for the conference to start.

I had a room set aside for deliverances, and I told them to put him in that room and make sure he didn't touch anything. I told them to wait. I went to another room, prayed, and asked what this man was dealing with. God said it was a spirit, a curse in the family, and it has been there for many years. Five people in the family were affected with the disease. God told me he needed to break and speak against the generational curse. I went to the man and said let's pray. While I'm praying, they are holding him down. Demons start manifesting and claiming the man. I kept pressing that Jesus now occupies this man's heart. I told them that they had no power and used the scriptures to drive out the demons. The real weapon is that when you talk about the blood of Jesus, the devil panics. Your own words mean nothing, so you must use scripture in a deliverance.

The guy was set free. They brought him breakfast, took him shopping for clothes, and then, in the afternoon, they took him to the meeting. He sat calmly in my meeting, which lasted a few hours. He was dressed up, fed, very calm, and totally healed.

I don't know how people can live without Jesus. How can people not believe in God? He's the one that holds your breath in your lungs. He's the one who gives you that opportunity to live.

The Woman in Labor

The day after I got permission to use the building, I was prepared. I thought maybe five people would show up, but the whole building was packed with people. I was amazed. We held meetings for four days. We started with 100 people but ended up with so many people that they had to stand outside. Many miracles took place. There was a woman who could not give birth. She gave birth to stillborn children twice. She was on the way to the hospital in labor with her third child when she heard the sound of worship and people testifying about miracles. Instead of going to the hospital, the people carrying her convinced her to go to the church. They felt like there was nothing to lose. I was praying for the people as they entered. Once they stepped inside, she screamed that the baby was coming! A bunch of girls crowded around her to create a wall of privacy. The woman gave birth to a normal, healthy baby right there! When the baby came out, it was a miracle. The mother gave the baby to me and told me to take the baby! She said she didn't want my baby to die! I had to convince the mother to raise the child for me and provide them with baby supplies so they would let me leave without the child.

When God Used My Shadow to Heal People

During the same meeting, a blind man accompanied by his wife entered. She led him in by holding one end of a walking stick. His eyes were stuck in position, with half-shut eyelids that could not be moved. A white substance protruded from the inside of his eye and covered it. I remember seeing him, but God told me not to lay hands on anybody during that conference. He wanted my shadow to heal people. When I heard that, I jumped to try and find where my shadow was! I told everyone to stand up and cry out to the Lord. My job was to make sure my shadow pointed to people. When I pointed my shadow at people, the people would fall down. I thought it was so cool!! My shadow fell on the blind man. He fell down, and I kept walking.

I heard him screaming, "Thank you for giving me back my eyes!" He asked everyone if they were the pastor because he didn't know what I looked like! He found me, and I told him to go to the altar, kneel, and thank God. I didn't touch anyone at all; I just walked around and pointed my shadow at them.

Later, I looked for the growth that fell off his eyes but couldn't find it anywhere. It makes me believe that God collects our pieces. The blind guy was healed completely.

There was another man with a swollen leg and foot. In Africa, we call it "Elephant Leg." It's swollen to the size of a person's body. There was an open wound covering the top of his foot. I was in the middle of the crowd, ministering to the people, and I made my way close to where he was. As soon as my shadow hit him, he fell to the ground. I kept ministering to people. As he describes it, it was like he was lying and someone was squeezing his leg, and as they squeezed, liquid came out. He was sitting in a pool of liquid from his leg. His leg, emptied, was now a normal size. The pain was gone. The skin on his leg was floppy and stretched. The open wound had shrunk to a small speck.

The Pastor Who Was Deaf

There was a pastor who had been pastoring for five years. After we finished that meeting, we went home. The pastor told me he liked me and the way I minister. He spoke very well. I was exhausted, so I didn't talk back but listened and smiled. He joined us after the service.

Then I said "Hey Manuel, are you coming back tomorrow?"

He didn't answer.

I said again "Hey Manuel, are you coming tomorrow?"

No answer.

I pounded the table and said "Hey! Manuel! Are you coming tomorrow??!"

He was startled when he saw me bang on the table. He realized I was trying to talk to him and said, "Oh, sorry! I can't hear! My ears don't work."

I exclaimed, "What do you mean by they don't work?"

He said that he lost his hearing.

"Aren't you a preacher?" I asked. "How do you serve the congregation?"

He told me that he reads lips. I became really upset at how the devil can make a minister who carries the Word of God deaf. I just jumped up, and without even asking, I put a pinky finger in each ear.

I rebuked the deaf spirit and said, "In the name of Jesus, receive your hearing!"

I pulled my fingers out, and he screamed like he was in pain. He then told me he could hear. I tested him a few times. Each time, he could repeat back to me what I said with perfect clarity. He was healed—just like that. Jesus can do big miracles and small miracles. It's the same God who does both.

Uganda Prayer Mountain

In Uganda, there is a place they call "Prayer Mountain." A Ugandan man bought this whole mountain because he felt called by God. People from all over the world lived in the mountain. They even established a church there, too. The people there were always worshiping. People would come together and worship corporately, and then they would separate and go into the bush to pray by themselves. The presence of God was so strong.

One time, while visiting Prayer Mountain, I cried out to God. I said, "God, I don't know what to give you? How do I fully surrender myself to you? How can I do it?"

Standing near a tree, I heard a deep voice speaking loudly. I thought it might be an animal. I looked up and saw a man in the tree praying! He was totally focused on his prayer to God. He told God that he wouldn't come down out of the tree until he heard from Him. He said he would become like a bird and live in the tree until God answered his prayers. It inspired me! I thought I needed to do that, too. I decided to give him space and find a place where I could cry out. I moved about a mile away and saw a woman in the grass, rolling around!

She was crying out to God, "Oh God! If you don't hear me, I won't sleep in my bed! I will sleep here in the grass! I can't do anything without you! I need you to be everything to me!"

First, I saw the man in the tree, and then this woman was rolling in the grass. I thought to myself, *WHOA!* I suddenly felt so empty. These people had so much to say to God. They didn't care what happened to them or how crazy they looked. They just wanted to get God's attention. When you seek God, you don't seek Him because you feel like it. You seek Him because He's your best friend. When you're close to someone, you can't ignore them. It doesn't matter if you're tired or hungry. You love that person and must spend time with them. From that day on, I cried out to God in a new way.

God spoke to me that day. He said "*Josephine, I will bless you. I will bless everyone who loves you, stands with you, and supports you. I will bless those you pray for. I give this blessing to you to pass to them.*"

When I left Prayer Mountain, things changed. People in my church started seeing God's blessings in their lives in many ways. They bought land and buildings, got better jobs, received full scholarships to schools, found spouses and got married, etc. People who the doctors told couldn't have kids started having kids! There were many miracles like that.

The Water Baptism and the Snake

During one of my visits to a village in Uganda, many people chose to follow Jesus and wanted to be baptized. The closest place to hold a baptism was a river about an hour's walk away. We woke up early to walk to the river while singing and worshiping Jesus. People would hear us singing everywhere we went and wanted to see where we were headed. By the time we arrived, there were 30 more people who had joined our group. When we got to the river, we felt these new people needed to hear Jesus! We had an altar call, and 37 people gave their lives to Christ and said they also wanted to be baptized. We taught about the meaning of a water baptism and the baptism of the Holy Spirit. After that, they still decided to be baptized. We started to give instructions on the process and what would happen. There were two big trees in the location where we were.

As we were about to get into the river and start, we saw a snake jumping from the tree nearest us and landing straight into the exact spot we planned to use for baptism. This was no ordinary snake. It was huge. It was about six inches wide, black in color, and impossible to miss. Everyone saw it fly from the tree and land in the water. Everyone gasped in fear. The crowd started to scatter. The pastor, who was supposed to go in the water to help me baptize, backed away and began telling people that the baptism was off. No one wanted to go in the water because of the snake. I felt terrible. It was such a long journey from the village, and we spent all this time preaching and teaching these people how to walk in faith. And now we're going to call it all off and walk away in fear? I felt something rise up in me. I couldn't let fear stop this baptism. I told everyone this isn't right, and I was going in the water for a baptism. I command everything in the water that's of the devil to die. I tell the snake it will not touch me in the name of Jesus. I told the snake if it came into the water to scare me or eat me, it would not be able to find my legs.

I walked into the water. Everyone watched. No one went in with me. I was standing alone in the water. I called out to the pastor and asked him to join me. He said no and walked even farther away from me. I called out to the people and asked them if they wanted to come because I was ready to baptize them. They said no. One guy piped up and said he couldn't go home without being baptized and would come in if nothing happened to me in the next twenty minutes. Twenty minutes passed and everything was fine. He walked into the water. I prayed over him and dipped him deep into the water.

When he came out of the water, I asked, "Did the snake get you?"
He said, "No!"
I said "How do you feel? Are you still scared?
He said "No!"
I said, "Good, stay here and help me baptize the rest."

When everyone saw that he was fine, and not afraid, they came forward to be baptized one by one. We baptized every single person there. The two pastors were the only ones who did not go into the water. After being baptized in water, everyone kneeled on the ground and sought God. They were all baptized in the Holy Spirit; some even spoke in tongues.

Remember to face your challenges. Your flesh will tell you not to do it, but the Holy Spirit will tell you that you can. I'm not saying to touch a snake, but you can do something that challenges your faith and believe that God will come through for you. James 2:18 (NKJV) says,

But someone will say, "You have faith, and I have works."
Show me your faith without your works, and I will show you
my faith by my works.

We put what we believe into action. Faith without action is dead. When you have faith, your faith is greater than anything.

Chapter 14

Miracles in Other Countries

When Pastor Joseph Resurrected

Joseph was a pastor in Namibia. He invited a group from the Bible School I was attending to preach in his church. We traveled for the whole day and got there around midnight. He was deep in the village countryside. That was Saturday night. We woke up early in the morning around 6 am to prepare for the 9 am service. This church was under a big tree. There was no building or roof, just the shade from the tree. As we're sitting on a bench, everyone shows up. Instead of starting with worship, Pastor Joseph began by standing up and thanking everyone for attending and then introduced us as the day's preacher. This surprised us, but the team leader of the Bible School agreed and got up to start preaching. The team leader spoke in English, and Pastor Joseph took the role of translator. They opened to John 1. The team leader read it in English and then invited Pastor Joseph to read it in the language of his people.

Pastor Joseph started moving his mouth like he was chewing, but no words came out. The preacher noticed something was wrong and tried to help by saying the first three words of the verse again, "In the beginning." Pastor Joseph repeated, "In the beginning," then the leader asked him to keep reading, but Pastor Joseph could not read anymore. He just kept repeating "in the beginning" over and over. Then he stopped, put his hands in his pockets, and started moving around, continuing the chewing motion as if he had gum in his mouth. We all were staring at him, confused. As he was chewing, I could smell food, but no one was cooking or serving it. But his mouth kept chewing as if he was chewing food. He could not say any words. I was looking at him, and I heard someone whisper, "Look in the tree," and a snake in the tree was slithering down. I told everyone to look, but no one else saw it but me. It didn't matter because as soon as I said that, Joseph fell down, and his head completely twisted around his body, facing backward, and he died with his mouth open.

Everyone in the congregation became angry. They turned to our group and started accusing us of killing the pastor and wanted to kill us. We didn't know what to do. The people surrounded us with sticks and rocks, crying and cursing at us. Some ran to get their knives. It was terrifying. They looked determined to kill us. Then I heard a small voice tell me it was time to pray. I told everyone to start praying, and the team started praying over Pastor Joseph, rebuking the spirit of death and praying for him to come back to life. After two hours, around 11 am, the Holy Spirit told me the tree was where witch doctors would come to curse the church. I knew we needed to take him out from under the tree. I lifted my head to share the message, and my eyes went straight to a man standing in the crowd. The Holy Spirit told me he was the witch doctor cursing the pastor. He was standing on the other side of the body. I yelled at him, accusing him of doing this. He gasped and panicked. He started running, so I started running after him! I chased him for a long distance and soon realized I should probably let the witch doctor go and head back to my group because I was alone in a new place. I turned around and ran back to the group.

We carried the body into the bedroom inside the house and put him down. We put people around the outside of the house to pray for intercession, and I was inside the room with the body and his wife. We prayed without stopping for hours. I would periodically encourage team members who were tired of praying to keep going. It was about 4:25 pm, and I asked God what else I could do. He told me to get water, pray over it, and put the water on his lips as a symbol of the blood of Jesus. I commanded the spirit of death to leave in the name of Jesus. The most incredible thing happened as I poured the water on his lips. His head, still completely turned around, instantly spun to the front. Achoo! He sneezed! Achoo! He sneezed again and then a third time! I yelled for people to come inside and hold him down. His wife was screaming. We kept praying until he finally came to his senses and woke up. When he did wake up, he woke up clear of mind, as if he had only been asleep. We were celebrating the victory of Jesus. Thirty minutes later, the wife stopped breathing. I knew it was demons we were dealing with. It was the spirit of death trying to have someone. She fell down to the ground. We treated her like we did her husband, prayed for her, and called for her to return. Within one hour, she was back.

This was a horrible day for us. There was no time to drink water or to use the restroom! We decided not to sleep because we were under attack. After the wife came back to life, we spent the rest of the evening worshiping, praying, and sharing the word. I started to teach about spiritual warfare and prayer. I told them demons were in this city. They confirmed that three witch doctors lived in the area. As we started to pray unified together, we prayed that we were covered under the blood of Jesus. We prayed and bound the evil spirits and did spiritual warfare. We saw fires from far away during our prayer in two separate places. We didn't know what it was. The following morning, news spread across the village. The homes of two of the witch doctors burned down that night. Everything had been totally burnt, even their idols. I asked the people why I smelt food when Pastor Joseph started behaving oddly. They told me that every time the witch doctors would get together, there would be the smell of food.

If you're reading this book, I want you to know that the Lord says *it's not by might, not by power, but by my Spirit* (Zechariah 4:6). When the Spirit of God leads you, things will be different. No matter what comes to challenge you, you can overcome that situation when you pray with faith, knowing that God is listening. Approach your prayers knowing that He hears and He answers. He's there for us and can even see into your future. Just go to him.

After that event, the whole village celebrated what Jesus had done! We led hundreds of people in that village to God. Even one of the witch doctors, whose house had burned down, came to us because he didn't know what to do next. We led him to Christ.

Jesus says to pray without ceasing. What if we had given up? We were tired, without water, breaks, or rest. What if we said it was taking too long? Think about the woman and the judge in Luke 18:1- 8. This story shows that even an unjust judge will dispense justice for those who continue to ask. How much more than would God, who is love, answer his own people.

Types of Prayer

There are multiple types of prayer. When you pray, you're talking to your father. God will pay attention to your words. Matthew 7:7 (NIV) says,

> *Ask and it will be given to you; seek and you will find; knock and the door will be opened to you.*

This is the prayer of asking.

There is also a prayer of forgiveness and repentance. You come before God when you want God to forgive you. You may feel discouraged and condemned. You want to start fresh. But before you ask for forgiveness, think to yourself if there is someone you've hurt. In Matthew 5:24, Jesus talks about the importance of making things right with your brother or sister. The Bible says to leave the sacrifice on the altar, go reconcile with your brother or sister, and then come back and give your sacrifice and ask. Then the heavens will be clear to you.

There is also a prayer of authority. It's the kind of prayer where you command. In Mark 16:17, Jesus gives us the authority to heal the sick and to cast out devils. Jesus himself has given us this. In Matthew 10, Jesus again gives us the authority to heal all kinds of diseases and cast out devils. You command because you have the authority in you. In Matthew 18:18-19, it talks about the power of binding. You bind the evil and disease in your body, you bind the situation, and then you loose the peace of God around you.

Then there is the prayer of thanksgiving. There are many ways to come to God with thanksgiving. David came to God with thanksgiving when he danced before the Lord, and he didn't care what people thought or heard about him (2 Samuel 6:16-22). Whether you come to testify at your church or just come to God personally, be sure to thank God for healing me! The Bible tells the story of the ten lepers in Luke 17:11-19.

Jesus healed all ten, but only one remembered to come back and say thank you. Maybe you were single and wanted to get married. When you find a spouse, don't forget to come back and thank God! Once you were renting, and now you have the means to buy a home. Don't forget to come back and thank God. It's good to come back with thanksgiving. After you pray and God answers you, what do you do? You say, "Thank you, God, for so much and for taking away my burden."

Finally, there is a prayer of friendship when you want to be in God's presence. It's when you give God all of your attention. You say, "God, I'm here before You. Let your will be done. Speak, and I will listen. I'm your vessel. Use me. I'm not here to ask anything else. I don't need anything. I just need you. The Bible tells the story of Samuel whose life was dedicated to waiting upon the Lord in the house of God. One night God called Samuel by name. If you wait upon God, you will see Him and hear Him.

When the Burundi President Invited Me to Speak

Burundi is a neighboring country to my home country. In 2004, there was a war going on. Rebels were killing people, and the Government didn't know what to do. The Government tried as hard as they could to end it, but people were dying in droves. One day, they decided to sit down and seek God to show them what to do about these rebels. As they were praying, God told them to invite me to Burundi, and I would teach Burundians about reconciliation. I had previously started a church in Burundi, but the Government didn't know me well. They tracked down one person who knew how to contact me. They reached out and invited me to speak at a conference. They gave me the details and covered my travel expenses.

When I arrived, they didn't know how to recognize me. They asked me what I looked like and what I was wearing. They told me to look for a big group waving flowers. I was so amazed to see this big group just like they had described, waiting for me. They picked me up at the airport in the President's convoy! That was SO COOL! They took me straight to the conference. The First Lady, who was in charge of the conference, was on stage, and when she saw me, she welcomed me in front of everyone. She said she was glad to see me, a woman of

God. She was so humble. I looked out at the crowd. It was all of the country's politicians, leaders, and officers, at least 300 people in total. I immediately felt so small. This was such a significant event. I had many thoughts running through my head. Why me? What do I have to say to these people?

They gave me the microphone, and I was so overwhelmed that I couldn't help myself. I burst into tears. Then, as I cried, I felt the Glory of God come over me. Then I heard a weeping—but not just my own. The people in the crowd started to weep as well. It was so unexpected. It was a move of the Holy Spirit. I finally pulled myself together and began to minister. As I spoke, God started pointing out specific individuals in the room and the situations they were going through. God showed me at least ten different people. By the tenth person, the crowd was amazed and praised God. In the end, I gave an altar call for anyone who wanted to give their life to Christ. Seventy people came to the front to give their lives to Christ. That was just the first day.

On the second day, they asked if I could go with them to march around the city to pray. We dedicated the city to God and prayed for the killing to stop. Only the women, accompanied by bodyguards, marched around the city. We walked the whole day until 4 pm, and at every mile, we would stop, kneel, and ask God to heal the people. We proclaimed that the war was over, and the country was washed with the blood of Jesus.

During that evening, the conference opened up to everyone. It was held at the big stadium and was overflowing with people. As the featured guest, they asked me to share the Word of God with everyone. After they introduced me, they gave me a microphone, and I started by giving a greeting. I opened by speaking about how honored I was to be invited by the President. After saying "thank you" to them, I suddenly felt like my mouth was filled with a new message to prophesy over the country. I looked out at the stadium and started to speak.

> "God is saying, in two months, the rebel leader will stop the rebellion and surrender himself, his army, and his weapons to the Government. He will be the next President of Burundi. He will be a Godly man, leading the people in a good and Godly way. The country will be at peace."

When I finished prophesying, I realized what I had said. I couldn't believe what I did. I thought they were going to kill me for what I said. I stood there, waiting for an arrest or some sort of backlash, but nothing happened. When I realized I was still alive, I finished preaching my message, closed the service, and headed back to Rwanda. Two months later, it happened exactly as God had said. The rebel leader surrendered his whole army and weapons. In 2005, he became the president of Burundi. This president began his term with worshiping and prayer.

Why do I share this? God speaks in every situation. We have to know God's plan. The Government prayed, and God told them to call me. When they invited me, I didn't have any messages until I arrived. Friends, I beg you to hear what God is saying to you. He can use people to speak to you, speak through you, or speak to you through signs. He will show you that He is with you. You are not alone. Psalms 34:4 says that God is with us no matter what is going on, and He will answer you when you are troubled and seeking help.

My Experience at Korea Prayer Mountain

A friend of mine took me to Korea to teach at Cho Yong-gi's church. While in Korea, my friend took me to a mountain that is dedicated to prayer. Yong-gi was inspired by his mother-in-law to establish his whole ministry, mountain and church included. As you approach the mountain, you can hear the nonstop rumble of people's prayers. Along the side of the mountain, underground tunnels lead to tiny rooms for prayer. The tiny rooms have been carved into the mountain. When you get there, you sign in, they give you keys, and you commit to being there for a time. You have to crawl in on your knees to get into the rooms. There is no space to stand, only space to sit or lay down. On one side of the room is a tiny table to put your Bible. Once they close the door, no one will hear you, and you can scream and be as loud as you want when you pray. I felt so inspired to see another culture on the other side of the world seeking God so intensely.

I signed into one of the rooms. As I'm kneeling and asking to see God, God tells me to come out so He can show me something. It was so peaceful and calm. It reminded me of when Elijah was hiding in the cave from Jezebel. God wasn't in the great wind or the earthquake. He was in the small, gentle whisper when Elijah came out of the cave. I came out in the evening around 7 pm. My friend went with me but had her own cave. I told her we needed to find something or someone. We went to the church associated with the prayer mountain. We came across a gentleman who had been at the mountain for two years. He refused to sleep on his bed; he fasted consistently. He was waiting to hear from God on something tangible. Hearing his story gave me a good picture of what Jesus referred to when he said to pray nonstop until God will bring His justice. It challenged me. Who would be willing to fast that long? Live like that for so long? That is real hunger. This man had spent two years sitting down.

There was another man who had been there for six months. He ran away from home because his family wanted him to marry a girl he didn't want to marry and wanted him to take up the family business. He didn't feel strong enough to do it on his own. God told me to pray for this guy's breakthrough, and God will give this son a new plan. This is part of living out your faith. If you have nothing left to look forward to, go by yourself to find a place to sit down and hear God. Being at the mountain made me feel amazed about what faith can do.

I went back to the Yong-gi's main church. It was filled with thousands of people. Yong-gi looked like the president of a town. I

Yong-gi's main church.

114

was amazed. It reminded me of the one righteous man who can heal the whole city. How does one person convince the entire city to follow Jesus? It must be God. When I entered his church, he was on his knees, praying to God during the worship time. During the testimony time, he was still on his knees. He stayed on his knees until they called him to minister. My spirit saw this and realized that it's all about God. It isn't because we know how to preach, nor because we know the Word. It's just the relationship. I returned to my home with a new realization of the ability of prayer to change things.

Chapter 15

Moving to the United States

A 10 Year Visa

I was fourteen when God first called me to go to the nations. Years passed, and I had no idea what that meant or how it would happen. In 2001, I was invited to preach at a Full Gospel Businessmen Conference in Rwanda. They wanted me to join them in Miami, FL, for a larger conference. I was one of thirty people they invited from Rwanda. We all went to the Embassy for visas. Everyone was denied except me and one other man. They gave the man a three-month visa. They gave me ten years. Ten YEARS! It amazed me! In my other travels, the visas I'd receive would be a month, a week, and sometimes only a few days. Outside of the conference, I had no plans to go to America. The moment they gave me a ten-year visa was the moment I realized that everything God had said to me would be fulfilled. When God has a plan for you, he will make a way to fulfill that plan. If you have a dream you have given up on or laid down because it has taken so long, I want to encourage you. Have courage and go forward. God will fulfill his promise.

The Jehovah Witness Who Came to Jesus

After the conference in Miami, I decided to visit a friend in Massachusetts. When I got there, I met a friend of my friend's, a recently divorced man. He was brokenhearted. He had come by the house to say hello. I saw he was on the verge of tears.

I told him, "Sir, I know someone who can bring you back to your feet and fix you."

He thought I meant someone like a doctor. Initially, he didn't want to hear me talk about Jesus as he was a Jehovah Witness, but he was so brokenhearted that he didn't have the strength to tell me no. As I talked to him, the Word of God began to soften him. He started asking me a lot of questions.

At the end of our talk, he said, "I'm in! I want to follow this Jesus. I want to know this Jesus. I'm ready for you to teach me!"

Every day for a whole month, he sought spiritual counsel. Eventually, he dedicated his life to Christ, received baptism in the Holy Spirit, and wrote a resignation letter to the Jehovah's Witness congregation. He pursued a Master's degree at Gordon Cornwall Theological Seminary, served as a chaplain in the US Army, and later established a church in New Hampshire. Today, he is a board-certified chaplain in a corporate setting.

Amos 8:11 says,

> 'Behold, the days are coming,' declares the Lord God, 'when I will send a famine on the land—not a famine of bread, nor a thirst for water, but of hearing the words of the Lord...'

Sometimes people are hungry but don't understand the source of the hunger. They eat, and they can drink, but they are still not satisfied. When the Word of God hits their heart, they realize they've gotten exactly what they've been seeking. After hearing the Word of God, this man was filled with courage. He was inspired to start a new chapter of his life. He had hope again. At the right time and right moment, Jesus kicked in. This man forgot his broken heart, and his life was totally changed. Revival always brings hope, confidence, joy, and the ability to love yourself again. Out of that love and joy, you have a desire to reach others.

My Best Friend Nadia

I spoke at a pastor's conference in Boston and made a connection with a Christian missionary school in North Carolina, who offered me a scholarship. Immediately after the conference, everything fell into place for me to attend. They enrolled me for the remaining two months of the semester, which felt like a divine appointment. During this time, God orchestrated for me to meet Nadia. She had a profound passion for spreading the message of Jesus worldwide and felt an instant connection with me from the moment we met. Her intense gaze on our first encounter caught me off guard. She said she could see Jesus in me and that there was something special in me. We became roommates and best friends. I used to leave the dorm in the middle of the night around 3 am. She would notice and follow me outside. She would see me praying and ask me to teach her how to pray. She would stay with me until 4:30 am praying and seeking God. More people heard about our prayer time, and we had about six students joining together with us. The time flew quickly. When the semester was over, I had to go back to Rwanda.

After I left, she was heartbroken. She felt like I left her behind. She returned to Oral Roberts University and, while there, found a scholarship for me to go to a neighboring school, Victory Bible Institute (VBI). She approached the church pastors overseeing VBI and petitioned on my behalf. It worked! She went to a couple she knew had a spare room and begged them to give me free housing. It worked! She contacted me in Rwanda. She told me about the scholarship and the housing. She sent me the paperwork I needed to fill out. Brave people can accomplish so much!

When I arrived, I didn't know anything about living on my own in America. Nadia made sure I lacked nothing. She gave me a cell phone, shopped for me, and let me use her vehicle. Everything she had, we would share. She taught me how to do makeup. She would order things based on what I missed from back home. I would give her my money and tell her I don't know what to get but to use it for our shared expenses. She didn't use it for our shared expenses. Instead, she would use it on me! She used it to help me acclimate to American culture. I would not have been able to come and study here if it wasn't for her. It reminded me of the scripture in Matthew 6:31 (NIV):

So do not worry, saying, "What shall we eat? Or what shall we drink?" or "What shall we wear?"

Nadia became a best friend. She learned my language and traveled to Rwanda with me to minister. We traveled to Uganda, Korea, and the US. At my wedding, she was my Maid of Honor. She honored me. I've never seen anyone treat me like she treated me. The Lord said he wanted me to train her as well. I enjoyed watching her grow spiritually during our time together. It is good to mentor someone who loves you. Because of our friendship, it was easy to share, and she would absorb everything I shared with her. It was easy to disciple her. I enjoyed seeing her grow. She became as gold, shining with the presence of God like it says in Isaiah 60:1 (NIV),

> *Arise, shine, for your light has come, and the glory of the Lord rises upon you.*

I miss her very much. My presence in America is because of her.

Through Nadia, God fulfilled the promise on my life. Because she brought me to Tulsa, I attended classes on the Oral Roberts University campus after Victory Bible Institute. God's purpose was for me to be prayed for by Oral Roberts and receive his generational anointing to Europe and Africa. God can bring someone into your life to help fulfill his calling on your life. If God has promised you something, he will fulfill it. As it says in Joshua 21:45,

> *Not one word of all the good promises that the Lord had made to the house of Israel had failed; all came to pass.*

The Barren Couple from Tulsa

There was a couple in Oklahoma. I lived with them during Victory Bible College. I stayed with them for one year, and they were so good to me. They were filled with the Holy Spirit and God's Word. There were scriptures displayed throughout their house. They gave me a room upstairs. Whenever I walked upstairs, I asked God why these strangers would give me such a beautiful room and place to stay! I didn't feel I deserved it. I asked God what these people need and how I could pray for them.

God said to me, "*They need kids. They cannot have kids.*"

For nine years, this couple was trying to have kids but could not, and the doctor did not know why. God told me to buy a new bed sheet and comforter to make the couple's bedroom shine. I didn't know how they would feel about me changing their bed! I felt embarrassed about entering someone's private space, like their bedroom, and replacing their sheets. I really struggled, but I knew I had to obey. I used my own money and made their bedroom look new and beautiful.

I hear the clear voice of God say to me, *"Lie down on the bed and declare 'It's done. You will have your own kids.'"*

I obeyed. After I got up, I was so embarrassed that I left before they got home and spent the whole night praying in the prayer chapel. I thought for sure they were going to come home and be upset about the bed. When I returned from praying at the chapel, they kindly thanked me for the new bedroom sheets set and cover. It was my last day with them, and I shared with them that God had a message for them.

I prophesied to them,

> "The kids you've been asking from God, you already have them, and that is the purpose for me putting the bedsheet and the bedcover."

I left for Rwanda, and after two weeks, she emailed me and said she's already conceived!

She said, "If I get a girl, it will be named Josephine, and if I get a boy, it will be named Joseph."

They had a boy, and he was named Joseph. They now have two boys! Isn't that awesome?

Meeting Oral Roberts

In 2003, God told me that He wanted to meet Oral Roberts. God told me that Oral Roberts would pray for me and I would receive his generational anointing to Europe and Africa. I had never heard the name Oral Roberts before. I asked everyone I saw if they had heard of Oral Roberts. Everywhere I would travel and minister, I would ask if anyone named Oral Roberts was at the service, but I never found anyone. Two years of asking went by without any success.

One day, while I was ministering in Uganda, I announced at the end of the service that I was looking for someone named Oral Roberts. A gentleman approached me with a magazine in his hand. He told me there was a man named Oral Roberts in the magazine. I was not convinced, but I took the magazine anyway and kept asking people about Oral Roberts. In 2005, while preaching in Denmark, an elder from one of the churches prophesied that the Lord would send me to a school, and I would receive the blessings God had prepared for me. He told me I should go home and pack my things because my time had come. I went home

to Rwanda and began praying. God told me to ordain people in my church and put everyone in a position to serve since I would be gone. I started to feel sad, realizing it may happen soon. It was not easy for me to leave because I felt the church would

Josephine ordaining pastors in her church in Rwanda before moving to the United States.

think I was leaving them behind. I felt like a failure. How could I go and leave my people and all the work behind?

God said to me, "*Your work is to obey My Word. This is MY church. I'm the one who died for it. Your job is to obey what I say.*"

After that word, I felt a lot of peace. I had no idea when I would leave or what school I would go to. I was just waiting on God. A friend of mine connected me to a school in America. Before I left, I hosted a party and announced to the church I was leaving and would be gone in two days! It was like dropping a bomb on them. The love was so strong in the church. We did such great work together, and I could see their hearts were broken. I could only answer their questions by telling them God had an assignment for me. I told them there were people who God had given me the responsibility to reach and that I wouldn't be able to if I didn't leave. In September 2006, I left my country for the United States.

As I arrived in Tulsa, OK, I knew I would meet Oral Roberts. I was elated! One day, while walking around Oral Roberts University, God told me to fast for twenty-one minutes and intercede for the university. I would circle the campus every evening, praying and blessing the school. A few weeks later, Oral Roberts came to visit. He spoke during the student chapel service. After sharing, he gave a general blessing but did not lay hands on anyone specifically. He was then escorted to the office behind the chapel. My heart sank. I thought I had missed my chance to be prayed for. I thought I should run after him to see if I could touch his jacket. God told me not to chase after him because God had already told me Oral Roberts would pray for me. As the other students were leaving, I saw Pastor Sharon Daugherty, my pastor from Victory Church in Tulsa, and ran to her. I knew that Pastor Sharon was a Godly woman full of compassion.

I said, "Pastor Sharon! Can I say something, please?"

She stopped and stared at me.

I said, "While living in Rwanda in 2003, God told me Oral Roberts would pray for me, and I would carry on his generational anointing to Europe and Africa. I've been praying to see him. I thought today he would call on all students to be prayed for. Would you please help me see him?"

Pastor Sharon led me to the room where Oral Roberts was. Now, you have to understand there was a serious security protocol. Pastor Sharon had to explain the situation to the guards and when we got to his door, we waited. Someone came out of the room, and Pastor Sharon asked for permission, and Oral Roberts agreed. Let me pause here and say that Pastor Sharon is my hero! She helped lead me to my destiny! They brought me into where Oral Roberts was. When they opened the door, I ran in and knelt at his feet.

I said, "Man of God, I have come from far away. God told me in 2003 that I would meet you. It's now 2009, and I'm here. I don't know how I got here, but God made it so. Man of God, I'm here now!"

He looked down at me and responded, "Something good is going to happen. Glory be to God!"

He took both of his hands and cradled my head. When he touched me, it felt like a heavy wind blew and shook me from my head to my feet. The next thing I could remember was lying in the chapel by myself!

I was worshiping, crying, and praising God. For two full weeks, my body shook with the power of God.

I believe God has many ways to meet your needs, speak to you, and fulfill what he promised you. I'm here to encourage you to wait upon the Lord. He will let everything he says to you come to pass.

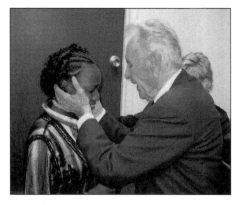

Oral Roberts praying for Josephine in 2008—a fulfillment of a prophetic word given in 2003.

Chapter 16

Closing Remarks

It makes a difference when you have Jesus in your heart. When you receive Christ, the Word is planted in your heart. Then, you must give Him the authority to take over. You need to submit your life to Him and tell Him that your life is His. That prayer becomes the foundation of your faith. In welcoming Jesus, it means you are born again. You're a child of God from that point on. You're a new person. Your name is written in the Book of Life. You become a citizen of heaven because of your confession. When you pray that kind of prayer, you dedicate yourself to Him. You accept what God has for you.

I hope this book has been a blessing to you. No matter where you are in your life, God is not done with you yet. You may be sick; you may be having financial difficulties, or you may be brokenhearted. Maybe you've been waiting for God to respond, and nothing has happened yet. Don't give up. There's nothing too difficult in this life when God is in the center of your heart. May God bless you, shine upon you, and reveal Himself to you. Amen.

About the Author

Since she was just 14 years old, Josephine has devoted her life to serving God with unwavering dedication. Over the years, she has traveled to 29 different countries, passionately preaching God's Word to diverse communities.

Throughout her remarkable ministry, Josephine has established 19 churches across various nations, witnessed countless lives transformed through her prayers, and prophesied visions that have come to fruition.

Josephine Mukamazimpaka with husband, Fred Ngabirano, and their 12-year-old daughter, Josie.

Josephine Mukamazimpaka and Fred Ngabirano married in 2009.

Her journey is a testament to the incredible ways God has worked through her obedience, manifesting His power through her inspiring testimonies, miracles, and wonders.

Since 2009, Josephine has been

happily married to Fred Ngabirano, and together they have a 12-year-old daughter who has also embraced a love for the Lord. The Ngabirano family has recently moved to Southwest Florida, where they are excited to continue their mission to serve and uplift the community in this new chapter of their ministry.

Check out "Meet My Spiritual Doctor" podcast with host, Sarah Nardella.